GRIEF, GRACE and HOPE

The Autobiography of
Pakisa K. Tshimika

Good Books

Intercourse, PA 17534
800/762-7171
www.GoodBooks.com

Photographs supplied by the author.
Cover photo by Wilhelm Unger.

Design by Cliff Snyder

GRIEF, GRACE AND HOPE
Copyright © 2009 by Good Books, Intercourse, PA 17534
International Standard Book Number: 978-1-56148-652-6
Library of Congress Catalog Card Number: 2009008401

Library of Congress Cataloging-in-Publication Data
Tshimika, Pakisa K.
    Grief, grace, and hope : the autobiography of Pakisa K. Tshimika / Pakisa K.
Tshimika.
        p. cm.
    ISBN 978-1-56148-652-6 (pbk. : alk. paper) 1. Tshimika, Pakisa K. 2.
Congolese (Democratic Republic)--United States--Biography. 3. People with
disabilities--United States--Biography. 4. Traffic accident victims--United
States--Biography. 5. Mennonites--Biography. 6. Mennonite World Confer-
ence. 7. Human rights workers--Congo (Democratic Republic)--Biography.
8. Human rights advocacy--Congo (Democratic Republic) 9. Kajiji (Congo)-
-Biography. 10. Fresno (Calif.)--Biography. I. Title.
    CT275.T9225A3 2009
    967.51024092--dc22
    [B]   2009008401

CHRONOLOGY OF THE LIFE OF PAKISA K. TSHIMIKA

June 2, 1952: Pakisa Kamwamba Tshimika is born in Kajiji, Congo, the son of Isaac Mutondo Tshimika, a Mennonite Brethren (MB) pastor, and his wife, Rebekah Natala.

October 1973: Leaves Congo to attend Fresno Pacific College, an MB-affiliated school in Fresno, California.

July 29, 1976: In a car accident near Medford, Oregon, suffers severe spinal injuries that leave him mostly paralyzed. He begins several months of surgery and rehabilitation in hospitals in Medford and later, in Fresno.

November 1976: Returns for the first time since his accident to the Fresno Pacific campus, where with the help of friends, he resumes classes.

Summer 1977: Returns to Congo with his "adopted" American parents, Wes and Ann Heinrichs, after graduating with a bachelor's degree in public health from Fresno Pacific.

Spring 1980: Graduates with a master's degree in public health from Loma Linda University in California.

July 1980: Following a solo trip across Europe, returns to Congo, where he meets Linda Kroeker in Kajiji.

June 17, 1984: Marries Linda Kroeker in Wichita, Kansas.

Fall 1987: Begins studies for a doctorate in public health at Loma Linda University.

June 1991: Receives doctorate from Loma Linda University; younger sister Tshamba dies in Congo.

January 1992: Returns to Congo to work with MBMS International, the MB mission agency, and the Congo MB Church. He remains with MBMS International until 2001. He also works with the public health organizations DESADEC, helping establish public health centers, and Memisa International.

April 1993: Death of older brother, Marc Mandjolo Tshimika, of liver cancer in Congo.

October 1995: Death of father in Congo.

1999: With colleague Tim Lind, begins holding Global Gift Sharing workshops in Africa for Mennonite World Conference (MWC).

June 2000: Older brother Tshinabu dies in Paris, France.

2001: Younger brother, Wally, abducted in 1990 by Angolan rebels, is killed in fighting with Angolan government forces.

February 2002: Death of older sister Suzanne in Congo. Later that year, joins MWC as associate general secretary.

March 2002: Becomes an American citizen.

May 2002: Death of mother in Congo.

2002-present: Continues work with MWC and other church-related agencies, and as an advocate for women who have been victims of sexual violence in war-torn Congo.

Introduction

The author Henri J.M. Nouwen, who died unexpectedly in 1996, could have been writing about my life in this passage from his book, *Finding My Way Home: Pathways to Life and the Spirit*, published in 2001.

"One of the most radical demands for you and me is the discovery of our lives as a series of movements or passages. ... You live all these passages in an environment where you are constantly tempted to be destroyed by resentment, by anger, and by a feeling of being put down. The losses remind you constantly that all isn't perfect and it doesn't always happen for you the way you expected; that perhaps you had hoped events wouldn't have been so painful, but they were; or that you expected relationships that never materialized. ... The question is not how to avoid loss and make it not happen, but how to choose it as a passage, as an exodus to greater life and freedom."

Nouwen's reflection brought back memories of a time many years ago when I went to Paris, France, to bury my brother, whose sudden death opened many old wounds. Two of my siblings had died early in life and I never knew them. In 1991, my younger sister, Tshamba, seven months pregnant, died from sickle cell anemia at the age of 25. Then, in 1993, my oldest brother, Marc Mandjolo Tshimika, died of liver cancer, leaving behind his wife and four children. My wife, Linda, and I later adopted three of them.

Our father, Isaac Mutondo Tshimika, died suddenly in 1995, shortly after I returned to my native Congo from six months in the United States. I never made it home in time for his funeral because of poor road conditions. Then, my younger brother, Wally, who was abducted in 1990 by rebels from the National Union for the Total Independence of Angola, or UNITA, was killed in 2001 amid fighting between UNITA and Angolan government forces. Two years later, my older sister, Suzanne, and my mother, Rebekah Natala Tshimika, followed them into eternity, leaving me only with my youngest brother, Samy.

I reflected on the pain of losing my loved ones, while my own life was spared following a serious car accident in 1976. That accident left me quadriplegic, confined to a wheelchair. After several months of rehabilitation, when many people thought my life was over, many miracles happened. Almost three years after the accident, I was finally able to walk with the help of a cane. Still, I never got back to the level of running after a soccer ball, as I once did with considerable skill in high school and college.

I continue to live a life of paradox—a life filled with blessings and yet with its share of pain and grief. I prayed to God for a good spouse and he gave me one, and yet he didn't bless us with biological children. I prayed for God to bless my professional life. He did, and yet my Congolese passport became almost a curse when it came to traveling in Europe and many African nations.

One day in my hospital room at Fresno (California) Community Hospital, my friend, Beka, brought me a poster that read, "When life gives you lemons, make lemonade." That poster opened my eyes. Everywhere I turn now, I see others afflicted with special problems and challenges. They are willing to share their stories with me and I am beginning to share my stories with them. I also meet those who allow the sour taste of the lemons they've been handed to control their lives.

This book would not have been written without the encouragement of Merle and Phyllis Good. Several years ago, while Phyllis was interviewing me for an article for Mennonite World Conference, she asked if I had ever thought about writing my life story. In spite of my excuses about my writing skills, she and Merle still believed I could write this book myself. I am grateful to them and to all the other family members and friends who supported me in sharing my story.

So this is my life—a life of grief, and yet full of grace and hope.

CHAPTER 1

The Death of My Brother

1999–2000

"Have a seat, please. I'll make room for you." The young woman made this offer as I got on an Air France shuttle taking us out to our aircraft at Charles De Gaulle airport in Paris. "Thank you. It is very kind of you," I replied as I sat down next to her. It was June 2000 and I was headed home to Fresno, California.

I hadn't slept well for several days. I wanted to cry, which is what I had been doing for the two weeks since I had come to Paris. Without saying a word, she took my hands and held them as I told her why I was in France.

"I came to bury my brother, who the French police say killed himself in a train accident," I said. "They refused to do an investigation or autopsy to determine the actual cause of his death. His wife didn't ask for one either."

The young woman told me she was traveling to San Francisco and Los Angeles with her teacher, a lecturer on death and dying. "I'll look you up on the plane because I have a book I want to share with you," she said.

After dinner, the young woman gave me the book. We visited for a long time. I could tell she listened from the heart and I felt I was with a fellow African—present in time of grief, yet not feeling obliged to say much.

I told her about my years working for church and relief agencies. I told her about my family life, including our three adopted children. Annie was studying social work at Fresno Pacific University, Patience was adjusting at Roosevelt High School, and Matondo was still in Kinshasa, Congo, where we were working to obtain official travel documents to bring him to Fresno. My wife, Linda, whom I had married in 1984, had a good job working for an agency serving the elderly.

My brother, Tshinabu, whom I had come to Paris to bury, was five years older than I. He was my biggest defender when we were growing up. No one harmed me because the other

kids in Kajiji, my hometown in Congo where I was born on June 2, 1952, knew my brother would beat them up. Even when I went away to high school in Kikwit, about 300 miles from home, I still felt safe because Tshinabu was already there.

Tshinabu went to France for the first time in 1972 to study theology at the Protestant Theological School of Vaux-Sur-Seine. After graduating, he continued his studies at the Catholic University in Paris, where he obtained two master's degrees in philosophy and management and

The author's brother, Tshinabu, right, with his father, Isaac, in 1994 in Kajiji, Congo.

a doctorate in philosophy. He always hoped to teach philosophy at the university level. That was his first love, and teaching was his passion. But getting such a position wasn't easy in France, which had a very tight selection process for a very limited number of teaching slots.

For about a year, Tshinabu and his wife, Isabelle, had been having marital problems. I wanted to help them reconcile, but the French consulate in San Francisco delayed granting me a visa. Instead, Tshinabu and I talked on the telephone quite often. One day he called to inform me that Isabelle had moved out with their children. He didn't know where they were. Soon, he became depressed and started contemplating suicide. He especially missed his youngest daughter, Aliénor.

He had some contact with his two older children, however. Without telling their mother, they stopped by the house to see their father each day before returning to the hotel where they were living. But the longer Tshinabu went without seeing Aliénor, the worse his depression became. A couple of weeks after Isabelle left, Tshinabu took an overdose and was hospitalized for several days. We talked many times while he was in the hospital. We had agreed he would leave the house to his wife and children until they decided whether to reconcile or divorce.

Tshinabu called me on my birthday, June 2, as he always did. We talked about our mother and our young brother, Samy, who was in Kinshasa. I promised to come to France to help sort things out as soon as I heard from the French authorities. But I never made it.

On June 10, five days before Tshinabu's birthday, Isabelle called me around 10 p.m. All she could say was, "Pakisa, it is Tshinabu. What am I going to do with the children?" I knew something had happened to my brother. I dropped the telephone and broke into tears. My big brother was gone.

Several days after my brother's death, I finally received my French visa. I was angry. It was too late. Tshinabu was gone, and my visa was only good for burying my brother.

Isabelle and two of the children met Linda and me at the Paris airport. Our cousin, Kaputu, and an old family friend, Lukala Charlie, were also there. The trip from the airport to my brother's house seemed longer than ever, although it was only 45 minutes away. When we got there, the house felt cold. Isabelle told me one of her sisters was in town to assist her, but that she was waiting for me to plan the burial details.

"Do you organize wakes or church services when someone dies in your family?" I asked the two sisters. As we continued to talk, it became obvious that Isabelle didn't see any need for a special service, but would go along with whatever I organized.

Late in the afternoon, Linda, Kaputu, Charlie, Isabelle, her sister, and I drove to the funeral home to discuss the arrangements. Friday was a holiday, so the funeral director told us we had to wait until the following Tuesday for the burial. In the meantime, we agreed to hold wakes during the weekend at Kaputu's house. We worked on the program and informed Tshinabu's friends and colleagues about the time and place of the funeral. It was good to have Linda beside me. She held my hands as I cried whenever I looked at my brother's pictures or saw his children. She also helped Kaputu and me plan the service.

We met at Kaputu's house for three nights. I took two of Tshinabu's children, Jean Sebastien and Sarah, with me, telling them how many friends their father had and how much they loved him. Several people came each evening. They each shared about their relationship with Tshinabu and what he had meant to them. Several said that Tshinabu had helped them save their marriages or deal with other conflicts.

On Tuesday, several of Tshinabu's friends from the Catholic theological school and colleagues from work came to the funeral. Larry Miller from Mennonite World Conference drove from Strasbourg, France. Neil Blough, an old friend of Tshinabu's, agreed to preach. Before the service, Larry, Kaputu, Charlie, and I drove to the funeral home. I wanted to see my brother's face. The police had discouraged me from this because of the extent of the damage to his body. He had been hit by a train. The funeral director agreed. "I would not encourage you to do so," he said. "I want you to keep positive images of your brother in your head." Larry, standing next to me, encouraged me to follow the director's advice. Suddenly, I started sobbing and could not stop. They loaded the coffin into the hearse, and we drove to the church.

A short service was held at the cemetery afterward. We invited the mourners to join us at the house for a short reception. I spent the next few days with Isabelle and the children reviewing pictures, letters, and papers that Tshinabu had written. I selected a few pictures I wanted duplicated, and Isabelle had copies made before I left for California. By Thursday, two days after the funeral, I was very tired, emotionally drained, and ready to go home.

My new friend on the plane could not hold back her tears as I recounted my brother's death and funeral. After a couple of hours, my friend left. I tried to sleep, but couldn't relax. My mind continued to wander as we quietly cruised at 39,000 feet. I thought the whole experience had been a bad dream. It was only a movie, I kept telling myself. I will see my brother again. I tried to forget the pain, but it wouldn't go away.

I was angry at Tshinabu. Why did he have to die at such a young age, leaving behind three beautiful children? Why didn't God stop him? And why did God spare my life in 1976 after my car crash, just to let me watch all my family members die?

CHAPTER 2

You'll Never
Walk Again

1976

I had just finished speaking at a conference on HIV and AIDS in Fresno, California, when my assistant, Heidi, drove me to the station to catch a northbound train for San Francisco. I was scheduled to travel that evening to Indonesia, to meet my Mennonite World Conference colleague, Tim Lind, for a workshop we were conducting on gift sharing. When the train's departure was announced, Heidi helped me get my luggage onboard. We said our goodbyes and the train started moving. A few minutes later, the conductor offered to assist me with my luggage as soon as we arrived in Emeryville, where I needed to transfer to a bus for San Francisco International Airport.

As often happens, a woman across from me said, "Sir, I see you're walking with a cane. Do you mind if I ask you why?"

I wondered where to start. I told her I had come to study in the United States with the goal of going to medical school. After that, I wanted to go back to Congo, then still known as Zaire, and work in our small hospital in my hometown, Kajiji.

We also talked about how my entire life had changed one July morning while I was driving to British Columbia to attend a college classmate's wedding. She wanted to know more details about how the accident happened, who was with me, and how I went from being completely paralyzed to walking with a cane.

It all started on July 28, 1976. I worked a late-night shift at an emergency veterinary clinic in Fresno. That night I worked with Dr. Gentzler, a wonderful person I always enjoyed working with. I had told Dr. Gentzler I was traveling to British Columbia for a wedding and that I'd be back at work the following week. Around 7 a.m. on July 29, we said goodbye and I left for home.

I was staying that summer with my "adopted" American family, Wes and Ann Heinrichs and their children. They had taken me in after we met at church, not long after I arrived in Fresno. After eating breakfast, Ann encouraged me to take a long rest before leaving that evening on my trip. I slept for a long time, then woke up midafternoon to finish packing for the trip. As soon as I was done, I took a long shower and was ready for the journey.

Around 7 p.m. July 29, two of my colleagues from school, Teresa and Linda, arrived to pick me up. We picked up a fourth passenger, Sheri, near Sacramento and soon we were on our way. The drive after Sacramento was beautiful. I had taken it before, but this time was different. I knew the road and I was traveling with people who also were familiar with the country.

I started driving from Sacramento because I loved to drive on long trips. Teresa, whose car we were in, sat right behind me. She had been my neighbor on campus. Our apartment was next to hers, where she lived with three other young women. We were going to the wedding of one of those roommates, Laura.

We stopped at a restaurant soon after crossing the Oregon border. I went to purchase gas while the girls ordered food. A piece of apple pie and a good cup of coffee were all I needed to get me going again. Before long, Linda and Sheri were sound asleep and Teresa offered to drive when I was tired. "I usually feel sleepy when the sun starts coming up, especially if I have been driving all night," I said.

"We can either stop in a rest area or I can drive when the sun starts to rise," Teresa suggested.

Then: "How are you doing, Pakisa?" Teresa asked me a few minutes later.

"I am OK so far," I answered. She began massaging my shoulders and neck.

That's the last thing I remember.

~

"Pakisa, you were in a very bad car accident," a parent of one of my college friends informed me. I could see from their eyes they had been crying. I didn't remember how long I had been in the hospital. It was hard to believe, but true. I felt like lifting my hand to shake theirs, but I couldn't. I tried to move my legs, but they couldn't move either.

"You broke your neck during the accident," said one of my friend's parents. It was then I became aware that I was paralyzed.

Later, when another person who was in the accident told me what had happened, I realized a series of miracles had occurred.

Miracle one: The accident occurred only a few miles north of Medford. As a result, it didn't take very long for help to arrive and take us to the nearest hospital.

Miracle two: A truck driver southbound on Interstate 5 noticed the taillights of our car and wondered why I had used the brakes on a flat section of the freeway. He parked his semi, crossed the divider, and saw our tire marks on the road. Our car had flipped over several yards from the freeway. He checked our car and as soon as he noticed a lot of blood flowing over my body, he radioed for assistance. Less than a half hour later, we were taken to the hospital in Medford. That truck driver was my first angel.

Miracle three: A neurosurgeon was visiting the Rogue Valley Hospital in Medford that week and had an excellent surgical team that could treat my spinal cord injury. Within a week, my broken vertebrae, C-5 and C-6, were fused, and I was ready for long-term rehabilitation. This doctor was my second angel.

Miracle four: I am told that I wasn't speaking English when we arrived at the hospital. This created a dilemma for the staff because they could not understand what I was saying. Someone figured out I was speaking French. Soon, they were able to locate an off-duty nurse who could speak French. She translated for the doctors and the other staff members. She was my third angel.

The Heinrichs family and the Fresno Pacific administrators were contacted right away about the accident. Soon after the news got to Fresno, Wes and Ann Heinrichs and their daughter, Marcia, drove to Medford to be with me. They brought a motor home, which they parked outside the hospital for whoever wanted to see me.

Despite my injuries, I could not feel alone because I was very fortunate. My family in Africa had assured me before I left Kajiji in October 1973 that I would never be alone, no matter where I was. God had provided me a home away from home in Fresno through the Heinrichs family. Fresno Pacific also provided me another home. But Medford, Oregon? How could I find a home and comfort there?

But the news of my accident seemed to touch the Medford community. Members of a local Presbyterian church visited me each day. Some brought flowers and others stopped by for short visits. A pastor from a Baptist congregation almost an hour away came to see me. I remember him lying on the floor of my room each time he came to see me, because the nursing staff had me facing down, immobilized, on a striker frame. He was faithful in his visits until I was transferred back to Fresno. I felt I had been visited by an angel each time this man of God came to see me.

CHAPTER 3

The Road to Rehabilitation

1976

Following the accident, I would need additional surgery and therapy if I ever wanted to return to college or try to be partially independent. These treatments required considerable money. I only had health insurance from college, which wouldn't cover much. I wasn't eligible for county, state, or federal aid because I was a foreign student. Friends and other people in Fresno were trying to find ways to assist me.

One option was to send me back to Congo. Several people who had done medical work did not support that idea because they knew medical conditions in Congo were not sufficient for my needs. Sending me back to Congo essentially was a death sentence. One doctor said that back home, a urinary tract infection most likely would take me first. Others suggested lobbying U.S. authorities to give me permanent status in the country so I could qualify for state and federal assistance.

I could tell I was still myself when my neurosurgeon walked in my room to discuss my forthcoming spinal fusion surgery. He came in when I was face-up on the striker frame. He first asked me if I understood the extent of my injuries and their impact. Then he explained the kind of surgery he was going to perform to fuse my broken vertebrae.

"What kind of incision are you planning to make on my body? Is it going to leave a big scar on me?" I asked. I could not see him well, but I'm sure he was wondering what the big deal was about a scar if it meant saving my life.

"Are you concerned?" he asked. I could hardly move my head, but my brain never stopped.

"Oh yes, I'm very concerned. I have a beautiful body that my parents gave me. I wouldn't want it to be ruined by anything," I jokingly told him.

"If you are that concerned, I think I have an idea," he said. "Rather than making the incision on the back of your neck, I'll do it from the front and follow the natural curve of your neck."

Today no one can ever tell where I had that first surgery.

Gary Nachtigall, dean of students at Fresno Pacific, flew to Medford to help with arrangements needed for my medical care. In Fresno, he had been working with the media, keeping them updated on my condition. He also coordinated fundraising activities. I was facing down on the striker frame when he entered my room. He lay on a mattress that had been placed on the floor and held my right hand for awhile. I could not squeeze or even feel his hand.

"Tshimika, my man," he said. "Your skin color inside is just like mine. Hey, we are the same!"

This was the man who first welcomed me to my new home at Fresno Pacific. In addition to being the dean, he was the athletic director and my geography teacher. Last time we had seen each other, I could still walk. Now, I was completely paralyzed.

Gary brought me good news. A rehabilitation center had just opened in Fresno. Leon S. Peters, after whom the rehab unit was named, promised to cover any treatment costs that funds raised by the college and the community didn't.

Arlen Gerdes, a missionary to Congo who was on home leave, requested permission from the MB Mission Board to stay longer so she could visit with me for awhile. It was wonderful to have Arlen in Medford. She was one of the people who sponsored me to come to North America.

It was so good having my American "sister" Marcia Heinrichs in Medford as well. She bought a little ball that she put in my hand and assisted me in squeezing. Each time she was with me, she sat next to me and held my hands, then put the ball in my hand and squeezed it.

Rogue Valley Hospital had a physical therapist on staff. Once I was stable, she did basic range-of-motion exercises for my arms and legs. She also wheeled me in my striker frame to a balcony and told me what she saw outside. She also took time to read the cards people had sent me.

One day, the therapist took me to our usual place on the balcony, then asked what my concerns were since the accident. I told her I wasn't really concerned about my physical condition. I was more concerned about not having children than anything else. I like children and had dreamed of having three who would play soccer or volleyball. One time, she suggested that if for some reason I never had my own children, my future wife and I could always adopt.

Before my accident, I had been blessed to have two friends on campus who were in wheelchairs. Anne was from Canada and worked in our college business office. I never heard her complain during the two years I had known her. Many times, I pushed her in her wheelchair on our way to church, a few blocks from campus.

Tom had broken his neck and had the same level of injury as I did. When we became friends on campus, he was driving a car specially designed for him. I knew one could live with physical limitations, but I didn't know if I could live with not being able to have children. The therapist was a good listener. She didn't pretend to have all the answers. However, we had time to talk about questions that other people were not asking me.

One afternoon, several weeks after the crash, I was told that arrangements had been made for me to move to Fresno to start intensive therapy. To help, a local businessman offered to charter an airplane to fly me there.

Leaving the hospital was a relief. After all the paperwork was finished, nurses prepared me for the trip and my physical therapists stopped by my room to say goodbye and to wish me well. Ann Heinrichs and Arlen flew with me on the twin-engine Cessna jet back to Fresno.

CHAPTER 4

Welcome Back to Fresno

1976–1977

"Are you ready to face the reporters?" one of the pilots asked me. "I guess," I answered. The pilot went on, telling me about all the people he saw as we taxied toward a spot on the Fresno airport tarmac where an ambulance was waiting. "They even have a red carpet for you, Pakisa. You won't see it but it will be under the stretcher," the pilot said. A few people approached the aircraft and transferred me to an ambulance stretcher.

After we moved a few yards away from the aircraft, we stopped and I noticed several microphones in my face. "Hi, Pakisa, I am a reporter for Channel 30 Action News here in Fresno. We have been following what happened to you. What is your hope now?" the reporter asked.

I could see my whole life marching in front of me as I reflected for a few seconds. I remembered the last night in Kajiji just before I left for the Congolese capital, Kinshasa. My family spent time singing and praying before going to bed, just as we had done since I was a baby. That night was different. I was leaving home with the intention of studying in Kinshasa, but also with a possible chance of going to the United States. My mother could not hide her tears as she prayed for my upcoming travel. Just before I went to bed, she reminded me of something she always told me each time I left home to go to high school in Kikwit.

"Pakisa, remember that we committed you in God's hands since you were a baby and he has always been with you," she said. "He will never forsake you. There might be times when you will not hear from us and, as much as we love you, we might fail you, but God will never fail you."

Finally, I answered the TV reporter. "My hope is in God, who had opened the door for me to come and study in this country," I said. "God will use me even if I am paralyzed and confined to a wheelchair."

I am not sure if I was asked another question that day. Slowly, we left the airport and I was taken by ambulance to Fresno Community Hospital, my new home for intensive physical, occupational, and recreational therapies.

Several reporters had gone ahead, so when I arrived at the hospital they took additional pictures that they showed during the evening news. My hospital room was on the sixth floor facing north. Medical staff wheeled me to the nursing station. I could hear them talking about my accident and the event at the airport. Some of them were saddened by what had happened to me. One staff member approached me and said hello. "We'll take good care of you," she assured me. "Don't worry about anything."

The door to my room was open and a tall gentleman walked in. "Hi, I am Dr. Holmes," he said. "Welcome to our rehabilitation center. I will be your physician while you are here. I heard that you were a good soccer player at Fresno Pacific College. We'll do the best we can to make your stay a good one, and I am looking forward to working with you."

He told me about the different services that were available and the initial assessment the staff would conduct in the coming days. Dr. Holmes became a wonderful friend and comforter. It had nothing to do with his knowledge of medicine, but with the way he conducted himself with me as his patient. He reminded me of the true traditional healers back in Congo, people skilled in providing remedies for different illnesses. Their best assets were the personal relationships they built with the people they helped. Dr. Holmes never failed me during my almost three months in the hospital, or when I returned for outpatient therapy.

As soon as he was gone, a very tall woman entered my room. Maybe everybody working in this hospital is very tall, I thought to myself. Then again, I was lying down and almost a month had passed since the last time I stood on my feet, so everyone seemed very tall to me. I had started to feel short although I was six feet tall.

The tall woman's name was Peggy and she was to be my physical therapist. She explained to me the different activities and the schedule I was going to be on. She also informed me that Janet would be my occupational therapist.

Therapy started the following day. Two sessions were scheduled each day, in the morning and afternoon. Progress seemed very slow and frustrating at times. I had no feeling below my neck and I only had a dead body for my therapist to work with. Peggy was very patient. I think it helped that I had been an athlete. Discipline and not giving up were part of the game plan. A few weeks later, I discovered Peggy was a Christian, so it became easy to talk about spiritual matters without either one of us fearing to offend the other.

Dr. Holmes came to see me early each morning, except on weekends when he was off. Our conversation usually started about the news from TV that morning. I didn't have much to do, so watching TV was my pastime.

It was 1976 and the Summer Olympics were being held in Montreal. This was the first time I had spent so many hours watching the different Olympic events. I watched gymnast Nadia Comăneci from Romania earn seven perfect scores. This was an Olympic first, yet she didn't show much emotion. In spite of this, she introduced me to the beauty of gymnastics. I watched that event during the whole competition.

I met Barb when we were talking about the Olympics and gymnastics with some of the volunteers during one of my therapy sessions. She was on the gymnastics team at California State University in Fresno. She took me to several of her gymnastic competitions after I left the hospital, which I enjoyed very much.

As I got stronger and more stable, I was allowed to visit my American family on Sunday afternoons. Their daughter, Sonja, and her husband, Norm, lived next door to her parents, so we spent considerable time together whenever I was home. Their first child, Heather, was born the year of my accident. Sonja placed Heather on my chest for as long as Heather was comfortable being with me. Heather didn't know it, but she made me feel normal.

Eric, Norm and Sonja's second child, was born in 1977, and each time I visited them after I left the hospital, Sonja brought out both kids so I could spend time with them. Sonja and I talked for a long time while I held Eric in my not so stable arms, and watched Heather play in her grandparents' back yard. Sonja made it possible for me to feel like myself and become normal again. She didn't appear to be afraid of me dropping the baby and helped me gain confidence in what I could do.

Sonja is very sensitive to other people's pain and struggles. We cried many times together as we visited. She used to come watch me play soccer in college and knew how much that sport had meant to me. I felt as if I were with a kindred spirit when I was with her. I promised her that one day I would take her to Kajiji to see where I had grown up.

Several of my former school colleagues came to visit me in the hospital. I had spoken with one of them, Beka, about whether to stay in the United States or go to a very prestigious medical school in France. "When God closes a door, he usually opens a window," she told me a couple of weeks before my accident. She walked in my hospital room a few months later, sobbing. "Pakisa, this is not what I meant when I said God will open a window if he closes a door." We cried together and before she left, she gave me a poster that read: "When life gives you lemons, make lemonade."

Dr. Holmes usually sat on my bed each time he came to my room. Dr. Holmes used a three-pointed pin to test my feeling in the different parts of my body. The reaction was always the same—no response. But with time, I started to regain some feeling, starting in my upper body. Then one morning, I told Dr. Holmes I had felt tingling in my feet during the night.

"Let's see," he said. He pricked the bottom of my right foot, and the foot retracted. He tried the left foot and got the same response. He pinched my right toe and I could feel the pressure. His face broke into a smile.

"Pakisa, your foot is responding to stimulus," he said. "That's a great sign." I started crying. I had been told a couple of months earlier that I had no chance of recovering. Now, I could feel my sensation improving each day. These small changes were part of the larger miracle of being able to walk again.

I also noticed great improvement during physical therapy. After a little more than a month in the hospital, I could lift my legs slightly. The range of motion exercises for my arms also started to produce excellent results. The occupational therapist designed fork, knife, and spoon handles that allowed me to feed myself. For the first time since the accident, I started feeding myself. My first trials were a mess. I didn't have much coordination and my arm muscles were still very weak, so sometimes I missed my mouth and food splashed all over my gown.

I was determined to feed myself. I was getting tired of being fed by someone else all the time. Sometimes I wasn't done chewing and whoever was feeding me already had more food ready to shove into my mouth. I began to understand why little babies and children make such a big fuss when being fed by their parents.

When the fall term started at college in September, I asked my science professors whether I could take a class in the hospital. Logistically, it was nearly impossible. I was able to move my hands, but not well enough to hold a book or turn pages by myself. One day, I told my occupational therapist that if she was as smart as she let on, why couldn't she design something that would allow me to hold and open a book?

Meanwhile, Dr. Isaak, one of my science professors at Fresno Pacific, agreed to allow me to take a class in the history of biology, which didn't require any lab work. If I could read the textbook, he would give me oral tests in my hospital room.

And Janet accepted my challenge. Each time I was in the gym for therapy, we talked about different gadgets that could assist me in gaining a semi-independent lifestyle. We also challenged each other on less serious things, such as when she told me that one of her friends was a very beautiful TV reporter. I told Janet that if her friend was so beautiful, then she should tell her to come for a visit. Soon, Denise Boucher came for the first of many visits. She also did a couple of television reports on the progress I was making.

Working with someone skilled in woodwork, Janet had designed a board that fit across my bed, and which could tilt however I wanted. They also designed a space that securely held a book and added an L-shaped lever with soft clay at the end. With a little pressure on the lever, the clay grabbed a page and turned it. It worked and I gave Janet a big kiss on the cheek to say thanks. I started my class on time and got a B-plus, which I considered a triumph.

Meanwhile, Fresno Pacific leadership, local churches, and youth groups were busy raising money for my medical bills. Scott, the son of my genetics professor, brought his piggy bank with all the money he had been saving for Christmas presents. He gave it to the finance department and told them he wanted to contribute toward my expenses.

Jerry Koop was a great cyclist who suggested a bike-a-thon to raise funds for my expenses. By then I was sitting in a wheelchair, so my therapist, Peggy, took me to the campus for the bike-a-thon kickoff. The local media covered the event, which once again made me realize how much the community cared for me. The event started with tricycle races. The college president, professors, support staff, and students participated in the event, which raised several thousand dollars.

Many other activities were organized as well. Little children I had worked with during summer camp organized a soccer tournament with the proceeds sent to Fresno Pacific on my behalf. There was also a sad story associated with one of the fundraisers. A young man in his late 20s decided to organize a basketball tournament to help with my expenses. The day before the tournament, he went to practice with several of his friends, collapsed suddenly, and died. The tournament was cancelled. That was very painful news for me to receive. Here was a young man who died trying to assist someone he didn't even know.

Other activities included a soccer tournament and a fundraiser held during an evening meal on campus. Diners, including more than 150 students, faculty, and staff, paid an extra $5 to go toward my expenses.

By late October, three months since my accident, my future looked more hopeful. We even started talking about the possibility of my leaving the hospital. But where would I go? I needed assistance almost 24 hours a day. The college decided to fix up an apartment to fit my needs, provided they found a couple of students to live with and take care of me. Once again, God provided. Randy, a 6-foot-8 former basketball player at Fresno Pacific, decided to move on campus and take care of me at no cost beyond his own living expenses. Two former soccer teammates, Doug and Tim, also decided to help. They received a quick orientation and training at the hospital on how to care for a quadriplegic.

Meanwhile, the college adapted the doors, bathroom, and furniture in one of its apartments. Wes Heinrichs built a desk suited for a wheelchair and placed it in my bedroom. By late November 1976, I had moved back to the Fresno Pacific campus.

CHAPTER 5

Living with a Physical Handicap

1976–1978

All things considered, life in an American hospital is relatively easy. Everything is done for you and many services are available. Going home and returning to a suddenly strange environment presented challenges. I started to notice the curbs on streets, the steps in people's homes, the beautiful but slippery rugs in bathrooms, coffee or tea cups I could no longer hold, the high and often fall-inducing bathtubs.

Even refrigerators were no longer as accessible as before, and bookshelves in the library now seemed much taller. In spite of these challenges, I was happy to be back on campus and to start my new life.

I was able to acquire an electric wheelchair, which made things much easier. The occupational therapy department at the hospital designed a board to place on my wheelchair for writing, reading, and eating meals. Janet, my occupational therapist, also worked with me about learning to write again. She suggested that if handwriting was impossible, I should consider learning to hold a pen or a pencil with my teeth.

Just before I left the hospital, a gentleman from Southern California called and offered a wheelchair that I could use when the electric wheelchair wasn't practical. With two wheelchairs, my host family in Fresno, three great friends committed to living with me, and the college community behind me, I was ready to face the world.

My primary caregiver, Randy, was very patient with me. Each morning, he helped me bathe and get dressed, made my breakfast, then got me in my electric wheelchair before I headed off to classes. Sometimes we must have looked funny to people in public. Here was a tall white man pushing a wheelchair with a black man in it. While out shopping one day, a little boy looked at us and in a loud voice said, "Look, mom, that black guy is being pushed by the white guy. What happened to him?" I could see the mother was embarrassed, but Randy and I just laughed and went on.

Other students on campus also offered to help. Several women students helped with simple chores. They took notes for me in class, washed dishes, and drove me places I needed to go. From time to time, our apartment was like Grand Central Station. In spite of my circumstances, I found a silver lining, as a young college male, in so many attractive young women coming to my aid. Their assistance was especially helpful for Randy and gave him time to do other things. Every once in awhile, Randy needed to travel early Sunday morning, so he assisted me with bathing and getting dressed. Two of our friends, Sharon and Laurie, helped me put on my shoes and get breakfast. Randy also taught me how to fall and get up again. He often asked, "What will you do if no one is near you when you fall down?" Well, it happened one day.

I was studying in my bedroom one afternoon, while Randy and several other guys were playing softball on the campus green. I made the mistake that day of not using my suspender, an elastic strap that held me against the chair each time I wanted to lean forward to get more comfortable. After reading for awhile, I forgot I didn't have the suspender on.

I leaned forward, and down I went. I screamed for help, but no one heard me. I finally fell asleep. When Randy came back about an hour later, he looked for me. He couldn't see me anywhere, but he saw the empty chair. He rushed outside to get the other guys.

"Are you OK, Pakisa?" Randy asked when he found me. They picked me up and saw I wasn't hurt. From then on, whenever they left me alone in the apartment, someone checked on me every so often.

I continued with physical and occupational therapy for a couple of months after I left the hospital. The hospital sent a van twice a week to pick me up and sometimes Randy went along for the sessions. My first ride to the hospital for outpatient therapy was memorable. That day, Randy got me ready and wheeled me to the van. Before I went onto the lift, the driver introduced herself by saying, "My name is Fanny, and I will take you for your outpatient therapy." I started laughing very hard until tears were running from my eyes. The poor driver couldn't lift me into the van.

The driver was African-American and she pronounced her name with a Southern accent and it just struck me as humorous. "What's so funny, Pakisa?" she finally asked me.

"What were your parents thinking by giving you such a name?" I asked her. "Did they want people to always remember your rear end each time they saw you or what?"

She also started laughing. "Hey, buddy, you better be nice because your safety depends on me."

I tried to control myself while she got me into the van and we started for the hospital. Each time Fanny showed up at our apartment, she instantly reminded me not to make fun of her name if I wanted to get a ride with her.

Soon, many other people started to get involved in my life. Churches began inviting me to share about my experience. It was always challenging to accept an invitation because I had to think of all the details of how my needs would be met. It wasn't easy for me to just let anyone assist me. I still needed help with bathing, emptying my urine catheter bag on my leg or assisting me with a bowel movement. Then at night, I needed to be undressed and have a bedside bag set up because I didn't have full control of my urinary system. I was comfortable with Randy, my American parents, and my other two friends, Tim and Doug, doing this for me. Anyone else had to excuse me, because I was still a proud Chokwe guy.

The first test of my modesty came when Barb asked if I could go with her to Concord in the Bay Area and speak at her church. I met Barb in the hospital while she was studying recreational therapy at Fresno State.

Many people from the church where she grew up were praying regularly for me. Some also had contributed toward my medical care. Randy wasn't available to travel on that weekend, so Barb offered to assist me. She reminded me she had emptied my leg bag a few times already, so why shouldn't I give her a chance to help with my other needs? She picked me up on a Saturday afternoon. Randy explained how to change my catheter and all the other special help I needed during the night, including how to place a couple of pillows between my legs and change my position a couple of times.

The weekend went well except for the humbling reality of letting a single woman, who was also younger than I, take care of my very intimate needs. The catheter became loose during the night and some urine leaked on the bed. I was embarrassed, but in the morning Barb told me not to worry about it. Barb's mother was a wonderful woman and never said anything about the incident. When I asked Barb about what her mother thought, she just said that her mom liked me and had cried during the night after we arrived. She thought of the pain my mother must be feeling, especially because both my parents were not able to come visit me.

One winter day, Barb took me for a drive in Sequoia National Park. We drove around for awhile and there was snow everywhere. That was the first time I had been in a snowy environment since my accident. My leg bag was full and needed to be emptied, so she pulled the car to the side of the road and suggested she empty it right there. "No, you can't do that," I told her. "We should look for the nearest bathroom."

"What difference will it make?" she asked. "There are no people around here anyway and the urine is not going to destroy anything." Soon after, she wheeled me into an open space with snow all around. Then she said, "Well, you are on your own. I hope you find your way home." She took a picture that she gave me later. A few months after, she helped organize my photo album and wrote under that picture: "Is this the way to Hawaii?"

The experience at Barb's parents helped me learn ways of accepting help from other people, even when it felt uncomfortable to do so. It wasn't something I could have accepted back in Africa. The clash of cultures became painful. I had to learn to accept assistance from women outside the hospital if I was going to live with my disability.

CHAPTER 6

Facing My Family

1977

Because my birth parents were not able to visit me while I was in the hospital or after, Wes and Ann Heinrichs, my American "parents," decided to accompany me to Congo in the summer of 1977, exactly one year after my accident. They decided to take me to see my family in Africa and on our way back do

The author's parents, Rebekah and Isaac, in the 1980s.

some touring—a safari in Kenya, a tour of the Holy Land, and a Mediterranean cruise, before visiting my brother, Tshinabu, in Paris. The planning went well and several friends pitched in for my ticket.

After we spent a couple of days in Kinshasa, Mission Aviation Fellowship flew us to Kajiji. It was on a dry and hazy August morning that we landed in Kajiji. Everything is very brown during Congo's dry season, which runs from mid-May to mid-August. People burn the wild grass to clear the way for hunting and the planting season. Sometimes it makes flying difficult because of poor visibility from all the smoke. A large crowd was waiting when we arrived. As soon as Wes, with assistance from the pilot, got me out of the plane, I noticed my mother and father approaching to welcome me. I turned my face away from them and held tight to Wes' chest and began to weep. Following local custom, women from the community poured white powder over my head while lamenting and crying. Finally, my parents reached me, and with tears in our eyes, we embraced for a long time.

My cousin, Mahungu, pushed my wheelchair for most of the time we were in Kajiji. Logistically, things were not easy, but we managed, thanks to Ann's creative efforts. Kajiji didn't have running water, so it had to be brought in from a spring in the valley. We had to be careful about how we used the little water we had in the house where we were staying. One day, sitting on my parents' veranda, I wanted to wash my hands before eating. My mother brought me a basin of water, and as soon as she saw I could not wash my hands by myself, she excused herself and asked Mahungu to hold it for me. I learned later she had gone to her room and cried for a long time. It was then she finally realized her son wasn't the same anymore.

On a Sunday afternoon, we drove to a village 15 miles from Kajiji, where one of my uncles lived. My uncle and his family, plus many others in the village, wanted to thank the Heinrichs family for taking such good care of me. My uncle was polygamous. His two wives and several of my cousins were excited to see us. As soon as we got out of our vehicle, they gave us a salute with guns. As in Kajiji, I was showered with more white powder. Many more tears were shed, and we were treated to a wonderful meal of pork, rice, plantains, peanuts, and fufu, a thick vegetable paste, before we returned to Kajiji.

Leaving Kajiji was hard, but I needed to return to the United States to continue preparing for my future. I knew now what was waiting for me in Africa whenever I came back as a person with disabilities. Even while we were visiting, my mind kept racing, thinking about how I would survive in a wheelchair in this place where roads were not paved and houses were not built to accommodate the disabled. I kept imagining my wheelchair stuck in the sand or having to hire someone to carry me when it was raining and the unpaved roads were washed out. But the more challenging I realized this place was going to be, the more I wanted to come back.

We left Kajiji with tears, just as when we had arrived. I was happy to have seen my family and to have reconnected with my mother, who had dreamed of my accident at the exact time it took place. She was told in her dream that I would be OK. However, she didn't realize how much damage the accident had done. At least now she knew who and what I had become, and how to pray for me.

CHAPTER 7

The Pain in My Brother's Face

1977

One thing you realize when you have a physical limitation is that many aspects of your life leave your control. On our way back from Kinshasa in August 1977, we stopped in Nairobi, Kenya, for only one day instead of the three we had planned, due to a delay in recovering my passport from Congolese authorities. The policy was for all Congolese nationals to return their passports to immigration authorities upon return to the country and to pick them up one or two days before leaving again. In a country where corruption was rampant, it was never a guarantee that one would get back a passport on time, if at all. Sometimes passports disappeared until you gave what was called *madesu ya bana*, or "beans for the children." For refusing to pay the bribe, we lost time scheduled for the safari in Kenya. Instead we connected with our flight to Tel Aviv for a tour of the Holy Land.

To visit Jerusalem, Bethlehem, Samaria, Jericho, and Capernaum was more than a dream come true. I could not believe that it was really me, a little kid from Kajiji, visiting places my childhood friends would never see.

From the Holy Land, we took a Mediterranean cruise and visited some of the churches described in the book of Revelation. I was so excited to be able to stand where the Apostle Paul had walked. While in Kajiji, one of the local carpenters made me a cane, which I took with me in the hope that someday I'd be able to use it for support. The taxi driver who drove us from the airport in Athens, Greece, dropped us at the hotel, then took off very quickly. Soon, we realized he had taken off with my cane. The hotel manager did everything he could to locate the driver. He called the police and radio and television stations, but the driver never came back. Although I wasn't yet walking, that cane was a sign of hope. Someone in my village had dreamed of the day when I might be able to walk again, and now that symbol was lost.

The Mediterranean cruise was fun. We arrived in Mikanos after dark. We had to leave the main ship and take smaller boats ashore. There was a narrow stairway that led to the small boat below. A couple of ship attendants offered to assist Wes and Ann in bringing me down. Things started well, but suddenly, one of the guys from the boat panicked and let go of the wheelchair. By some miracle, Wes held the wheelchair with one hand while Ann helped him regain our balance. It wasn't until later that we realized how deadly the whole scene might have been. The waters were dark, and I don't think they would have found me that night. God was good, and once again I felt my life had been spared for a reason.

From the Mediterranean, we went on to Paris, where we visited my brother, Tshinabu. The last time I had seen Tshinabu was in 1972, when he left to study in France. We had talked on the telephone several times after I moved to Fresno. He called several times to inquire about my condition following my accident.

Tshinabu and our cousin, Kaputu, were at the airport waiting for us. This was the first time I had visited the French capital. Although I didn't care much for the French people, Paris was a dream city to visit. When we were in high school in Kikwit, Paris meant intelligentsia, romance, art, and free thinking. Paris also meant excellent cuisine: hard bread and soft butter as well as fluffy croissants.

Paris was also a city I would have visited regularly after I was accepted to study in Lyon if the accident had not changed my plans. Now, I was in a wheelchair. But my brother was here. He used to take care of me when we were in high school, but I don't think he ever thought he would see me like this. Now he saw me in my new physical state. He couldn't hide his pain.

Wes and Ann realized that Tshinabu was having a hard time seeing me like this. They tried to reassure him that in spite of this, I really was fine. They hugged him and told him I had been in much worse condition before. We picked up our luggage and drove to his apartment.

The days we spent in Paris were wonderful. Wes and Ann had visited Paris before, but had a very negative experience. Now they were in Paris with people who knew the city, culture, and people. Tshinabu took us everywhere. We visited the Eiffel Tower, Champs Elysees, the Louvre, and the Latin Quarter. We visited his friends and many local cafés. I also enjoyed being in the company of our cousin, Kaputu. He had collected and recorded many Chokwe songs, and played them as we traveled in the city. He also shared Chokwe proverbs he had gathered as part of his doctoral research in linguistics. He was such a good storyteller that I could never have enough time with him. I wanted to listen to his stories all the time. They reminded me so much of our childhood back home.

While in Paris, I realized once again how small our world is. We were visiting Paris during the daytime and decided to stop for lunch in a small outdoor café. As we were getting ready to leave, a group of people who looked like American tourists stopped by the café and were looking for places to sit. They were speaking English. We greeted them and offered them our table because we were ready to leave. Sure enough, they were not only Americans, but also from Fresno. The man was a physician at Fresno Community Hospital. As we talked, the daughter remembered the story of my accident and soon the doctor and his wife did, too. We said goodbye and they took our place in the café.

Just before leaving Paris, we were invited to dinner by one of my brother's friends, a retired French army general. We were their honored guests that evening, so they offered us a toast with the best champagne from their family winery. But this offer was somewhat problematic.

"We don't drink alcohol," Ann said. Within a few seconds, the mood in the house changed completely. It became cold and the disappointment in our hosts' faces was evident. My brother explained to me in Chokwe that our refusal to accept the champagne had offended the family. I explained to Wes and Ann what was going on and suggested we drink the champagne and any wine that was offered. I said it would be very insulting not to accept their offer because my brother had meant a lot to them and this family wanted to thank them for taking care of me. We agreed to accept whatever drinks were offered. How things changed. The mood became festive again. They served the best wine they had kept for years in their cellar.

We still laugh about that encounter whenever we have a family gathering because when we arrived at my brother's apartment, we had to climb a flight of stairs. Wes supported me on one side and Tshinabu on the other, and up we went. We started singing as we climbed the stairs and Ann said we sounded like a trio of drunken sailors.

I didn't want to leave my brother, but the time came for us to go. Tshinabu and Kaputu drove us to the airport. There, with only two hours before our flight, I was told my passport wasn't in order and that I would have to go to the U.S. consulate in Paris to get a new visa. Otherwise, I could not board the aircraft. Because of the traffic, it took more than 45 minutes to get to the consulate. The airline promised to save our seats if we came back on time. We arrived at the consulate just before it closed for lunch, but the person responsible for signing the visa papers already had left. By the time we had all the papers we needed, it was too late and we missed our flight. We were booked on the next flight to Los Angeles. It was fine, except for one small complication.

We found all our bags back at the airport except for one. Unfortunately, it contained all my medical supplies. Back in Paris, Tshinabu and Ann tried to round up everything I needed for the night from local pharmacies, but some items, such as an external catheter, could not be found. From this experience, I learned not to keep important medicine and supplies in any of my checked luggage.

The following day, we left without any problem. On our way to the airport, I asked my brother to get a few baguettes to take with me to Fresno. I wanted to impress my friends there about my time in Paris. The baguettes survived the trip, but were rather dry by the time we arrived in Fresno more than 15 hours after they were purchased. We also found my missing bag in storage at the Fresno airport.

CHAPTER 8

The Daughter of an Immigrant Father

1980–2008

As I grew older, I began to feel more kinship with those whose families had, like me, moved around and never felt at home in a single place. I realized that my relationships with women had been affected by this world view. I developed many relationships with American girls while in college and graduate school, yet they all seemed to lack something. I guess I was looking for someone with an exile's mentality and lifestyle. Mennonite missionaries in Congo told us about their families moving from the Ukraine to North America. Some stayed in South America, in Paraguay and Uruguay. In college, most girls didn't talk about their parents' or grandparents' migrations.

I met Linda Kroeker in Congo in the summer of 1980. She was working at the Kajiji hospital and lived next door to my parents. I arrived in Kajiji that August when all the other missionaries had gone for their annual retreat in Kinshasa. Linda was the only missionary there when I arrived, because she recently had contracted hepatitis. People were not supposed to visit her, and she was very tired and needed to rest. Elsie Fischer, another missionary who arrived soon thereafter, went to visit Linda each day and brought her whatever she needed.

One day, I decided to visit Linda myself. I picked some yellow flowers along the way. How lovely it was, I thought, to give her flowers that matched her jaundiced skin. I didn't realize that those flowers bore the seeds of a long-term relationship.

Not long after I arrived in Kajiji, Linda was invited by my parents to attend a reception they organized for me. When I met Linda at my parents' house, I remember thinking how it was too bad that so many single missionary girls were destined to die as old maids.

When I first knew Linda, she was finishing a Christian Service assignment in Congo, but wanted to come back as a full-time missionary. Unfortunately, for me anyway, she was assigned to Kikwit, which was some distance from Kajiji.

I saw her from time to time whenever I traveled to Kikwit for meetings, and the only way we could correspond was by letter whenever there was a vehicle traveling between the two places.

At the time, I was coordinating all the public health programs for the church in Congo, so that gave me the chance to travel to Kikwit even more often. Still, visiting her alone was not an easy thing, because some of the other missionaries were not happy that I was spending so much time with her. Once I was told that one of the missionaries had written to the mission office back in Hillsboro, Kansas, to tell them that Linda and I were together too often.

Despite this, she would invite me to her place for dinner whenever I left Kikwit for Kajiji. Each time I ate at Linda's place, the cook, who was my cousin's husband, would remind me how wonderful Linda was.

"I know," was always my answer.

A couple of years later, I was invited to speak at a conference near Chicago. Linda asked me if I would like to visit her parents, John and Hulda, in Kansas. While visiting her family in Wichita, I found myself alone one morning with her father.

"Do you love my daughter?" he asked me. I wasn't sure how to answer. I hesitated for awhile. Back in Congo, a girl's father asking such a question usually meant he smelled trouble. But I wasn't in Congo and this was the first time I had met this family. I used to befriend many girls in California and their parents had never asked me this question. I think Linda's father could read my mind. Before I had the chance to say a word, he added, "You know, Linda writes about you all the time when she sends us letters. You must have made a big impact in her life. We knew about you from reading our church magazines, so it is good to have you in our home these days."

I felt relieved by this, and felt I then could answer his question.

"I actually like your daughter. We have become good friends," I answered.

John brought me a cup of coffee and told me about visiting Linda in Congo and how much they had liked Kajiji and the country. We talked about the current situation in the country and in the Congolese church. After a short silence in our conversation, he asked me a question I had hoped he would not. "Would you like to marry my daughter?"

Now I knew I was in trouble. This man seemed to like me and yet my mind kept thinking about stories I had heard about white people being upset when their daughters dated or married blacks. Would I be shot and tossed away or maybe sent to jail for saying I wanted to marry his daughter?

Part of me stayed very calm. This was a family who had sent their daughter to Africa, and even went to visit her there. They were Mennonite Brethren, as I was, so they must be good people. John didn't seem like a threatening person, and besides, I was a Tshimika and we Chokwe could handle anything.

I paused for awhile, and then answered his question: "I really like your daughter, but I would consider marriage only when I know that I will be fully accepted by your family and that Linda will be accepted by mine. I don't believe in a marriage of the couple only."

John was smiling as I answered his inquiry. He wasn't forcing me to marry his daughter. He was just curious about my feelings toward her.

John then recounted his experience of marrying Hulda. He was born in Ukraine and moved to North America with his family when he was a young boy. To some Mennonites who had immigrated earlier to North America, his family was alien and considered Russian. Some in the community resisted when he wanted to marry Hulda. But he said to me, "Look, we have been married for several years now and we have three beautiful daughters. I can imagine your fear or apprehension, but you shouldn't worry too much about that. I know the experience because I went through it myself. Make your decision and we'll support you."

What a relief it was to listen to his story. I felt at home and this was just like talking with my dad. I started to imagine a son and a daughter of immigrant fathers getting married. Things couldn't get any better than that.

A year later, on Sunday, June 17, 1984, Linda and I were married in Wichita, Kansas.

We were married by Pastor Roland Reimer of First Mennonite Brethren Church in Wichita. Among the guests were the Heinrichs family, their daughter, Sonja, and her husband, Norm; Dr. Roger Fast and his family; my former roommate, Randy; and Ted and Justina Friesen from Dinuba, California, whom I had gotten to know after my accident.

We wanted a simple wedding and that's what we had. Linda's mom made her wedding dress, a meal was served at the church for out-of-town guests, and an open house was held at my in-laws' home. We wrote our own vows and kept them secret from one another until the actual ceremony.

Photo from the wedding of the author and Linda
Kroeker in Wichita, Kansas, in 1984.

Linda looked radiant and more beautiful than I had ever seen her. On that Sunday morning, she became my wife and lifetime companion.

Pastor Reimer spoke on the story of Ruth. How fitting, I thought, because Linda and I both were children of immigrants, from Ukraine and Angola, respectively. But on that morning, Linda's people became my people and mine became hers.

After the wedding, someone asked my in-laws how they felt about their daughter marrying a black man from Africa.

"At least one of our daughters married a Mennonite Brethren boy," her father replied.

When they told us later about that conversation, I realized I had found another home through this daughter of an immigrant father.

By sealing the relationship with Linda, my life also gained Linda's two sisters, including Nancy, her older sister who had a son and two daughters. When we first met, I was not sure if Nancy would accept me as a brother-in-law. My doubt disappeared when she agreed to be Linda's bridesmaid. With time, Nancy became a wonderful sister to me. Now, whenever we are together, Nancy and I always end up discussing what life in heaven must be like. Maybe this is what dreamers do when they are together.

Nancy's husband, Reg Boothe, has been a great inspiration to me. Reg lost his first wife and two sons in an airplane accident caused by a maintenance problem. He is a survivor and a man of very strong faith. I once asked Reg why he did not sue the company that maintained his airplane.

"Pakisa, God blesses me in many ways, so why should I sue them for a few million dollars?" he said. "The money will not bring me back my wife and my boys. I know that those who had worked on the aircraft do fear that I might sue them one day, but I hope that they can be assured that I mean it when I say that it has never been my intention."

Linda's younger sister, Ellen, has a daughter and a son. Ellen and her husband, Gil, a Vietnam War veteran, were easy for me to connect with from the beginning. I like to listen to their stories of living in Alaska, where Gil worked as a bush pilot. More recently, they lived in New Zealand, where Gil worked with environmental issues. Beka, their daughter, traveled with me to Congo in January 2008. Their son, Peter, wants to be a sports journalist and attends Drake University.

Linda's parents, John and Hulda, visited my family in Kajiji in 1985. John taught several young men how to build cabinets, while he made some for our home. One of those men is still making cabinets, beds, and chairs for a living in Kajiji.

John died in 1997. His dying wish was to ask the U.S. government to help rebuild Congo instead of sending more military aid to its dictator. He even asked someone to help him write a letter to President Bill Clinton, pleading that medicine be sent to Kajiji, but John died before the letter was sent.

Hulda came to live with us in August 2001, and became the grandparent figure our household needed. She was gentle, with a great sense of humor. Hulda died on Christmas Day 2006.

Though Linda and I would try to have biological children of our own, we never succeeded. Even though I had sustained permanent spinal injuries in my car accident, this did not prevent us from conceiving children. Furthermore, fertility tests conducted on Linda and me turned up no problems. Despite this, after years of trying to have our own children, we decided that the costly fertility drugs and other treatments were not going to work and we gave them up.

But in the early days of our marriage, when I was still a student at Loma Linda and my wife was working as a nurse, those were probably the most troubling times we would experience. Many tears were shed as we tried to, but then could not, have children of our own.

CHAPTER 9

The Death of My Mother

2002

A few years ago, my flight to Denver, Colorado, had been delayed for a couple of hours so I spent most of my time visiting with a fellow passenger in the airport lounge. He was a retired farmer from Reedley, California, a few miles from Fresno. We talked about farming life and the impact of undocumented farm workers on the economy of central California. It is a topic that always interests me. In the central San Joaquin Valley, we enjoy the agricultural products, but some don't appreciate the people who make it possible to get the food to our tables. Each time I have an opportunity, I bring up the subject with farmers to get their perspectives. That day wasn't any different.

When we finally got on the plane, I sat next to a woman who was on her way to Florida. She seemed subdued. Her eyes were red and she looked like she had been crying for a long time. She looked so miserable I could not wait to ask her what she was going through.

Before I knew it, we had spent two hours talking about our mothers. I found out she had moved to Florida soon after high school. She was married to a well-established lawyer there and had come to Fresno to visit her ailing mother. She said she was concerned that each time she came for a visit and then left, it would be the last time she would see her mother alive.

We talked about the important roles mothers play in our lives as children and as adults. She wanted to know if my mother, Rebekah Natala Tshimika, was still alive. I told her my mother had died suddenly in May 2002. She forgot about her own pain and wanted to know more about what had happened to my mother. I still find it hard to talk about my mother's death because it left such a big void in my life. Even as an adult with my own family, I still feel like an orphan.

The author's mother, Rebekah, working in a manioc field in Congo.

As I looked back, I remembered how phone calls from Kinshasa to Linda's and my home in Fresno had started to scare us each time we received them. It seemed when someone called it was because a loved one was sick and needed financial assistance or had died and other relatives needed help for burial expenses. We were not very surprised when we received a phone call from Kinshasa informing us that my sister-in-law, Maka, the wife of my late oldest brother, Mandjolo, had died. We knew she had been very sick and wasn't expected to live much longer. The second phone call a few hours later, however, almost destroyed me completely. This time, it was my mother who had died, just hours after my sister-in-law.

My wife and I had received this kind of message before and each one got harder to swallow. While I was working on my doctorate in public health at Loma Linda University in California, in 1991, I learned that my younger sister, Tshamba, 25, had died in Kajiji. In June 2000, we had received a similar call from Paris when my brother, Tshinabu, died.

Nearly two years later, in February 2002, we learned my older sister, Suzanne, had died of a congenital heart condition that had not been diagnosed in time for her to receive any medical care.

This time, after my mother's and sister-in-law's deaths, we decided I would travel to Kinshasa with our two adopted girls, Patience and Annie. I wondered how I would comfort the girls during this trip when I had so many questions without answers myself. We all had lost loved ones and we continued to lose more.

Perhaps going back to Kinshasa would set me on a new journey to greater life and freedom. Our family's experience living in the Central Valley of California had shown us that during winter, even though the fog obscures the sun, the source of light is still there. It was this sun above the fog that my girls and I sought as we left Fresno for Congo.

Going back to Kinshasa wasn't easy. It had been 18 months since I had last visited there. For Annie, it had been nearly four years and for Patience, three. In the meantime, many things had changed in the country. President Kabila had been assassinated, and a second civil war was raging. The economic and social conditions had deteriorated dramatically. Furthermore, how were we to face all the little demands made by those who still thought everyone living in North America must be extremely wealthy? Despite all this, we went anyway.

Arriving at Ndjili airport was a positive experience. There were only the airline personnel, not soldiers, surrounding the aircraft. We saw airport police at a distance this time, and the soldiers were even farther away. It only took a few minutes to go through customs because our luggage didn't make the short transfer time in Johannesburg, South Africa. (We finally got all our bags after more than a week of going back and forth to the airport.)

Driving to my mother's house was the hardest part of arriving in Kinshasa. I was used to finding my mother on the veranda. If she was in her bedroom, she came out as soon as she was told I had arrived. If she wasn't sleeping, she usually was reading her Bible. This time the mood was different—very somber and with sadness in all the faces. A couple of cousins, my younger brother, two nieces, a nephew, and several friends of the family were waiting to welcome us. Several MB church leaders also came to greet and pray with us. Visits from friends and church leaders became very comforting.

A week after our arrival, we had an extended family get-together. According to our tradition, this was the time when any people who were not present during a burial are told about what took place. Close to 35 people were present for the event. It was decided that our time together would be spent not mourning our loss, but celebrating the lives of two people, my mother and sister-in-law, who had lived fully. We listened to the stories regarding my mother's final days, the night she had a stroke, the kind of health care she received, the funeral, and responses from the church community and the neighborhood where she lived. I could not help but feel frustrated, angry, resentful, betrayed, and joyful at the same time.

My mother had suffered a stroke at 1 a.m. the day she died, but my younger brother and a nephew, now studying in medical school, could not get any assistance from the small clinics near them. It wasn't until nearly four hours later that she was admitted at the general hospital in Kinshasa and another hour before even an IV was administered.

In one of the clinics, the doctor wouldn't even come out of the room where he was sleeping to see her. She died at 11 a.m., almost 10 hours after she had suffered the stroke.

The decision was made to bury her before my arrival, and the three MB conferences in Kinshasa organized the service. A local Christian and Missionary Alliance congregation also participated in the planning. Several hundred people gathered at the house the night before for a wake organized by the churches. Several choirs sang during the whole night, and one of the pastors led a short meditation and prayer every few hours.

On Sunday, when my mother and sister-in-law were buried, Maurice Matsitsa, my former assistant when I was working with MB Mission and Service International, played a tape he had recorded of my mother just a week before she died. On the tape, my mother talked about her walk with Christ, her prayer life, and her many years of marriage to my father. She also talked about death and why she looked forward to heaven, as well as about losing children and remaining faithful to God. The tape became the sermon at her own funeral. People applauded as if she were still alive.

I didn't realize how much impact she had on the lives of even the young people in the neighborhood where she had been living for only two years. The day before she had the stroke, she had walked around the neighborhood paying back money she owed to people. For some it was for peanuts, and for others it was for sugar or milk. In the evening, she gathered everyone in the living room for a time of prayer as she always did before going to bed. At the end of prayer time, she told my younger brother, my niece and her husband, and another nephew who was studying in medical school, about what she had done during the day.

"I don't owe anyone anything in this neighborhood or anywhere else," she said. "I paid all my bills and if someday I am not around and someone asks you to pay for something I had taken, you should not believe them."

My niece, Samba, asked her if she was expecting something to happen to her. "No one ever knows, so it is always good to be prepared," my mother said. My mother suffered a stroke a few hours later while alone in her bedroom and never spoke again.

When she was alive, she had visions of many events in other people's lives. She had revelations about the deaths of my siblings. She knew the exact time I had been in the car accident and the extent of my injuries. God spoke to her in dreams and revealed many future events. Her final revelation gave her peace with herself, other people, and God.

A couple of big vehicles were rented to transport people to the cemetery outside the city. A problem arose among the young people. They didn't want my mother's body transported in a vehicle to the cemetery.

"She is our mother and we must carry her to her last resting place," one of them said.

The cemetery was nearly 20 miles from the house and it was impossible to carry her body that far. After some discussion, the young people agreed to carry the body up to the main road, five or six blocks from the house. But once the coffin was in the hands of the young people, it became difficult to retrieve it. They decided to walk with her to all the places they knew my mother loved to visit. They stopped at the market and took her through the main streets where she used to walk and to different houses she used to visit. Along the way, these young people waved flowers and palm branches while singing in Lingala. Several others stopped the procession to pay their final tributes.

More than an hour later, they reached the main road, put the coffin in one of the vehicles, and finally released her body to church leaders and the immediate family for burial.

I told the woman on the plane that my mother didn't die alone and had not lived in vain. She was finally resting from all her years of hard labor, but her funeral showed that her legacy would continue.

CHAPTER 10

The Pain Returns

2003–2004

At the end of January 2003, while traveling in the Netherlands and France, I started to suffer from excruciating pain on the right side of my neck, in my right shoulder, and in three spots along my back. I thought it was due to long travel, a heavy schedule, and cold weather. The pain continued for the whole month I was in Europe. I had been able to walk with the assistance of a cane for some time, but this discomfort was overpowering.

On my way home, while at the airport in Paris, I suddenly felt a shooting pain in my right shoulder and numbness in my right hand. It became so bad I could hardly use my cane for walking. I felt paralyzed. I couldn't move. My right shoulder muscles felt very tight. I was having muscle spasms. I could feel big knots in my shoulder muscles and felt like crying, but didn't want to do so in such a public place.

Isabelle, my sister-in-law, and my niece, Aliénor, one of Tshinabu's daughters, had accompanied me to the airport that day. They asked me what was wrong. Aliénor offered to take the computer bag I was carrying. With my hands free, I was able to exercise and achieve some range of motion in my shoulder. The muscle spasm lasted for about five minutes but felt like an eternity. Luckily, my gate wasn't very far, so I ended up not requesting a wheelchair. After saying goodbye to Isabelle and Aliénor, I left for Amsterdam, where I boarded a transatlantic flight to San Francisco.

Upon my return to Fresno, I made an appointment to see my primary physician at Kaiser Permanente, my health maintenance organization. My doctor tried everything from physical therapy to strong pain medication, but without results. Three months later, she requested X-rays and an MRI. The results showed a cyst inside my spinal cord as well as a narrowing in one of the cervical canals. I was sent to the neurology and physical medicine departments for further consultations. In each case, both doctors suggested I see a neurosurgeon. The Fresno Kaiser does not have its own neurosurgeons so it contracts with a neurosurgery group elsewhere in the city. They only have limited consultation and surgery days at Kaiser, so getting an appointment was a challenge.

It became obvious I was going to wait for a long time for an opening at Kaiser. I sought counsel from several physician friends, including a cousin who works at Kaiser, about whom to consult. With the help of two physician friends, I got an appointment with the person they all recommended, Dr. Williams.

After reviewing the MRI and X-ray results, he told me he needed additional MRI testing, but from a machine with a better resolution. I told him I was planning to travel to Congo and Zimbabwe that summer, but wondered if it was wise for me to take the trip given the level of pain I was feeling. Dr. Williams said if I could handle taking the medication, I should go ahead with my plans and then call his office as soon as I returned.

When I returned from Zimbabwe the first week of August, I was able to get an appointment for September 30, 2003.

"This second MRI is much better than the first one. From what I see here, surgery is the only option," Dr. Williams said. The procedure clearly involved risk, including the possibility of collapsed lungs, coma, total paralysis, and death. Despite this, he assured me technology had improved so that most of these risks were minimal.

The surgery was scheduled for the afternoon of October 6. "It might take 3½ to four hours," Dr. Williams explained. I said hundreds of people all over the world were praying not just for me but for the whole surgical team. I told them I was at peace and I also asked them to feel at peace because I knew God was with all of us. Dr. Williams thanked me, gave me a big hug, and said, "Actually, the surgery won't seem like more than five minutes for you, but it will seem very long for the family members who will be waiting for you to come out of the recovery room. See you soon."

Following the operation, when I opened my eyes, I saw Linda standing next to my bed. Patience was leaning against the wall in a far corner. I wasn't quite awake, but I could feel a distance from Patience. I wondered if she was afraid that I was going to die. I vaguely remember saying "good night" and falling asleep.

The next day, I was more alert and could tell that I had lost some sensation from the neck down, especially on my back side.

Dr. Williams assured me that I would regain feeling, but that it would take time. He said that the surgery went very well.

"I will have the hospital physical therapist see you today and try to help you get up from the bed," Dr. Williams said.

Linda asked if I had any restrictions. After my early injuries, I lay on a striker frame for a long time and had to wear a hard collar to support my head and neck.

"Pakisa does not need anything special," Dr. Williams said. "He just has to be careful for awhile. I want him to start moving as soon as possible." He held my hand and said, "Pakisa, don't worry. Your head is not going to fall off."

I told the kids about our discussion with the doctor and about how I was feeling when they came to visit that day. I could see they were worried. Matondo hugged me, then stood by the window and asked if I'd be able to walk again. I assured him I was OK and that things would turn out all right.

When Patience came later, she still seemed distant. I asked her if she was scared. She didn't say much, but I could see she wasn't too sure I was going to recover.

Patience had suffered a series of tragedies in her life. She had seen my brother, her biological father, leave Kajiji for medical care. He didn't come back alive. She had hoped to visit my brother, Tshinabu, in France, and then we got the news that he had been taken to a hospital following a drug overdose. Less than a month later, he was killed in what was described as a train accident and possible suicide. Closer to home, Patience's best friend, Crystal, was killed in a car accident coming back from a football game near Fresno. After that, Patience became depressed and suicidal. She was hospitalized for a couple of weeks. The months that followed were very difficult for our family.

We prayed that God would bring healing in Patience's life. The pain of her suffering was excruciating for me. Each day that Patience was still alive was cause for rejoicing. One night, after Linda and I were already in bed, she knocked and gave me a little note with the following message: "Dear Father, it is 9 p.m. on Sunday evening. I've been trying to go to sleep since 8 p.m., but I am having trouble sleeping. All I can think of is not wanting to be here on Earth, Father. I can't see the point of living anymore. I try so hard to think about my purpose of being here. I don't see any. Well, I will try to go to sleep now. Love you, Patience."

Pain and death were all Patience had known in her short life. Why would it be any different this time? Several months later, she shared with me her thoughts in a note in which she revealed her fears about my hospitalization and surgery.

> *Dear Dad:*
>
> *"Hospital." Just the sound of it gives me chills. I was happy for you when you told me that you finally had a date fixed for surgery after a very long wait. But at the*

same time I was scared to death and very nervous. I was happy because you will be pain-free, and now you won't have to take those drugs anymore. I was scared to death because whenever someone that I cared for had gone to the hospital for treatment, they never came back. They went forever, and I didn't know what would happen to you because you are all to me and I didn't want to lose you. I don't know what I would do if you would leave me. It is very hard to think positively about losing a loved one when you have experienced so many losses. The night before your surgery, I prayed to God, even though I had been mad at him. I asked him to help you go through this surgery and come out of it alive. I also asked him to prove to me the opposite of what I was thinking at the time. I was very nervous about seeing you at the hospital that evening after your surgery. I didn't know what to expect. It was the first time for me to see you on the hospital bed. When you talked to me, I felt so much better and I knew that you were OK and the worst part was gone. I love you, Patience.

Following my surgery, I spent three nights and four days at St. Agnes Hospital, where I was treated like a king. I could have several visitors any time in my room. Many people from church came to visit and my friend, Dr. Fast, came often to provide moral support. I don't know if he realized it, but I could tell he was concerned. My pastor, Bill, also came to visit and brought me the news from church.

I always looked forward to seeing Sonja when she came to visit me after work. One night before I left St. Agnes, she brought her guitar and played and sang some of my favorite songs, including "Redemption Song" and "Buffalo Soldier" by Bob Marley and "If I Should Fall Behind" by Bruce Springsteen. With Sonja singing, I forgot all my pain. The hospital coffee was what my friends and I called "church basement coffee," where you needed close to 10 cups to get the full impact of the caffeine. As a result, Linda brought me coffee from home and told everyone at church that I would rather receive coffee than flowers when they came to visit.

On the second day in the hospital, Dr. Jonathan Wiens assessed my rehabilitation needs and suggested that, as soon as I was stable, I transfer to the San Joaquin Rehabilitation Center for two to three weeks. He also explained that rehabilitation medicine had improved so that patients are no longer kept hospitalized for months at a time.

Furthermore, he suggested that I remain open to staying longer if I progressed more slowly than I expected. I shared with him my concern of having Linda take care of me at the same time she was caring for her mother.

"I'd like to leave for home when I am able to take care of most of my personal basic needs," I told him. He understood. He told me not to worry and that he would work with me on it.

The day before leaving the hospital, I became very emotional about my situation. I started out in a good mood despite all the medications I was on. They had already taken me off the intravenous pain medicine because I could eat solid food and drink fluids. Later during the day, one of the nurses brought me two bouquets of flowers with cards, which she read to me. One was from Mennonite World Conference staff and executive board members and the other from an old college friend and his wife. Both cards spoke about what I meant to everyone, how they didn't feel that I belonged in the hospital, and that they considered me their hero.

After the nurse left the room, I started to reflect on the pain that so many people were feeling for me. I thought about my immediate family, especially Patience, and I broke into tears. I was still sobbing when Dr. Williams walked in. A few minutes later, Bill, our pastor, came in. I explained to both of them that even though I wasn't very concerned about my surgery, I now realized it had caused a lot of anxiety in the people who love me.

On the fourth day following the operation, I was moved to the San Joaquin Rehabilitation Center.

"Are you the Pakisa from Africa who went to school here in Fresno and was hospitalized after you were in an accident in 1976?" a nurse asked.

"Yes, that's me," I answered.

"You might not believe this, but I was one of your nurses more than 20 years ago," she continued. She went on to tell me that four of the nurses I had before were now working at that rehab hospital. She also said I was the first patient she had ever transferred from a bed to a wheelchair, and that I had told her not to be afraid because God was going to help her.

She had been going through a bitter divorce at the time and she found visiting me very comforting. She reminded me how we talked and how I encouraged her to move on with her life. In 1976, I had built my community around the doctors, nurses, therapists, and other patients in the hospital. Once again, my community was developing around some of the same people who had helped me feel at home before.

I was determined to get out of the rehab center as soon as possible and back to my regular life. I figured the only way I could do that was to work hard and push myself. Dr. Wiens cautioned me to be patient. He knew how much I liked my work and how I became impatient if I was staying in one place for a long time. He also mentioned the fact that I could make progress, and then experience a setback. I should be prepared for anything.

CHAPTER 11

Son of a Stubborn Father

1960s–2003

I guess the emotional time I went through before leaving St. Agnes Hospital was a sign of something much deeper than I had realized. During my second night at San Joaquin Rehab, I had a vision of my father, Isaac Mutondo Tshimika. He walked into my room and at first stood far from my bed. He was wearing a shirt and a pair of pants that I remembered having purchased for him when I was living in Kajiji in the 1980s.

"How are you, Dad?" I asked him. "I am fine," he answered. Then he moved closer and sat on my bed. He held my right hand very tightly. Then he told me not to worry because everything would be all right. He sat there for a long time without making further comments. I felt his hand sliding away from me as he bid me goodbye. I didn't want to let go. I grasped at his hand again, but he repeated the same thing. "Don't worry. Things will be all right. I have to go."

Unwillingly, I let his hand go, and he walked away from my bed and disappeared into the corridor of the hospital wing. I woke up and started laughing because in some way it reminded me of a similar vision several years earlier after the death of my sister, Tshamba.

Tshamba died in June 1991. I had last seen her the year before. We had talked about bringing her to California for studies. Our friend, Rachel, who teaches at the University of

California in Los Angeles, asked us if Tshamba could stay with her. She could help her with her Chokwe language materials before Tshamba started school.

However, in Congo, Tshamba got involved with a young diamond trader and she became pregnant. In the seventh month of her pregnancy, she began having a crisis with her sickle cell anemia, which she had suffered from for most of her life. We had always worried about her future marriage prospects. In settings without sufficient medical support, a pregnancy could be complicated by her condition. It was too late. The doctors didn't have time to even save her baby, and Tshamba died.

I was angry. I wanted to kill the young man who had gotten her pregnant. I was angry at myself because I wished I had taken my sister back to the States with me after my last visit to Kajiji. Two years later, she visited me one night in our apartment at Loma Linda. I had just fallen asleep when I saw her walk into our apartment. Even though all the doors were closed, I could see her pass through the wooden doors.

The author's sister, Tshamba, shortly before her death.

Just like my father did, she sat by my bed and held my hand and assured me that things would be all right. She informed me that she was no longer having pain and that I should stop being so angry. She asked me to move on with my life because she was fine. She gave me a hug and walked out the same way she had walked in.

~

As far I can remember from when I was a child growing up in present-day Congo, we nearly always had company at meals. Sometimes, our guests were people living in Kajiji who might have been visiting with my mother, my father, or any one of us kids. Other times, they were visitors from out of town—MB church leaders attending a conference in Kajiji, or leaders from other churches or communities who had been released from the hospital but were waiting to go back home. Sometimes we had people who, passing by, were invited by our parents to join us for a meal.

My family was not rich. Our home was very simple. Our living room furniture was made from bamboo or lumber from Shakalongo, my dad's village of origin. We had a couple of indoor bathrooms, but we did not use them for lack of running water. My dad did everything he could to make sure we all had mattresses on our beds. Someone would make mattress tubes that we filled with dried grass.

A small building next to our main house served as a kitchen. All the cooking was done on wood fires. All the children helped with the chores—fetching water and wood for cooking, or making coffee in the morning.

No matter how much food we had, there was always room for one more person at our table. We never went hungry despite the number of people sharing meals with us.

At a young age, we children learned quickly that hospitality in our home wasn't a matter of choice but a part of our family culture. It was our security. My brother, Tshinabu, found out the hard way when one day he refused to join us at the supper table. When I asked him to join us, he said he would eat later. My dad understood what my brother was up to. There were too many people in the house that evening, and Tshinabu thought he would not have enough to eat. He liked to eat a lot of meat like any young Chokwe man. He thought by not eating at the same time, a larger piece of meat would be kept for him. Dad told him that we would save food for him and that he should not worry about joining us at the table.

Soon after we finished eating, Dad asked Mom to fix a big bowl of luku, made from ground cassava flour, and a nice-sized piece of meat for my brother. Not long after our guest left, my dad sat by the dining room table and invited my brother to join him. Dad asked my brother to eat everything and not leave any sauce, meat, or luku. Tshinabu realized what was going on and started to cry. He tried to excuse himself after eating a little bit, but Dad told him that he wasn't done yet. When he could not eat any more, Dad took him to their bedroom and gave him a good spanking and made him promise never to avoid joining the family or our guests for a meal.

There also was room for one more in our bedrooms. When our guests needed space to sleep for a few nights, Mom and Dad always made sure our guests found a bed. Sometimes we shared beds with guests we knew, while other times we slept on the floor. Other times, someone who came to stay for only one or two days ended up staying a month or more. Most were people who came to the hospital but didn't have relatives in Kajiji, or young people from surrounding villages who were studying in Kajiji.

I remember inviting Isidore, who was in my third-grade class, to come home with me after school. After eating supper, he helped me do the dishes and I accompanied him back to the dormitory where he had been staying. He was living in a dorm for boys. They had to do their own cooking during the week, even at that early age, because there was no cafeteria for them at school. Isidore looked malnourished, so I kept inviting him to our place for meals. One day, I asked my parents if Isidore could just move in and live with us. They agreed to have Isidore join our family during the week and

The author's father baptizing in Kajiji in the early 1980s.

return to his family's village on weekends. Isidore lived with us throughout his primary school studies and also on and off until he finished high school. Today, Isidore is a schoolteacher in Kinshasa. He is only one of many young people who lived with my family as I was growing up. Many of these young people are leaders in the Congo MB Church.

When I worked in Kajiji, Kikwit, and Kinshasa, I often wondered why I had grown up in such a hospitable family. There is so much joy in being hospitable. At the same time, hospitality also brought pain and internal conflict. The same people my family hosted or helped later came to me for assistance. Many of them also wanted me to assist their children. They needed money, clothes, or school supplies. Some brought medical and utility bills and expected me to pay them.

Some were thankful, but others were not. A distant cousin once asked me for money to pay school bills for her kids, purchase medicine for her ailing spouse, and cover six months of utility costs. When I told her that I didn't have money that day, she reminded me of how great we were as kids and how my parents didn't discriminate against different family members or whoever else showed up at their house. I tried to explain that it wasn't a question of not wanting to help her, but that I just didn't have any money that day. She didn't believe me.

When attending a meeting in Kikwit, a man once asked me for financial assistance for himself and his wife, and scholarships for his children. As we visited, he kept reminding me how he had driven me to a mission hospital three to fours hours from Kikwit after I had contracted cerebral malaria during high school. I began to get scared because I started to realize that if this pattern continued, my own children would have to take care of two or three generations of people because of my family's hospitality. The cruel reality was that there was no turning back. Yet I still believe hospitality is not a choice, but a part of who we are. It was my sense of security and still is.

My mother was probably the embodiment of our family's hospitality. This was brought home to me when I talked once with Mama Masolo, wife of a former general secretary of the Congo MB Church. I had scolded Mama Masolo because she always had too many people staying in her home, sometimes indefinitely, and because she didn't always have enough food for her own family because of all the other people she was feeding. Her response was that when she was young, she had prayed she would become like my mother. My mother never kept things for herself, always had space for others, and never turned anyone away. This was a gift from God that Mama Masolo wanted to have.

My mother came to live with us in Kinshasa after my father passed on in 1995. We were living in a big house that was once used as a hostel for missionary kids. The MB Mission and Services agency had turned it over to the Congo MB Church. We used one section of the house, which had two bedrooms, and kept two apartments available for visitors. Our section had a big veranda where my mother used to enjoy spending most of her day when she wasn't in her room reading her Bible.

Each time I came home at the end of the day or when I returned from a trip, I always found her sitting on the veranda visiting with someone. "Could you please prepare something for our guest?" she usually asked one of our kids. It didn't make any difference how many people came by the house, she wanted to make sure no one left without something to drink or eat.

"This is my house now; I decide what we do," I once jokingly told my mom.

"So what?" she replied, laughing. "Your house or mine, people who come to your house cannot leave hungry or thirsty." We laughed about it and I told her that she had won that discussion.

Most memories of hospitality in my family were very positive. However, a couple of experiences have taken me time to process and come to terms with. A pastor from another mission station was staying with us while he received medical care at the Kajiji hospital. As we did many times, after supper we sat around the table to visit and talk about everything and nothing. It was a family time, when we asked our parents many questions about life.

One night while this pastor was staying with us, we started asking questions about why the MB missionaries taught people that it was a sin to drink alcohol. We reminded our father about the story he once told us regarding the time of famine in the region and how many people survived on palm wine. He told us that each morning the men went into the forest to harvest the first wine, which was sweet, for women and children. Later, they brought back the more fermented wine for the men. With limited staple food, palm wine and corn-meal provided some relief for the people until food was either brought in or there was a good harvest. My dad told us about the danger and consequences of drinking alcohol. He said that from his own perspective, drinking wine wasn't a sin. However, he also told us stories of people who abused alcohol and what happened to their family lives.

Dad also talked about people lying after having consumed alcohol because of the fear of being excommunicated from the church by missionaries. My favorite story involved one of his cousins who was caught smelling of alcohol by a missionary. Our uncle had been drinking with his buddies in a secret place. On his way home, he met the head of the mission station. This missionary, having smelled alcohol on my uncle's breath, asked him if he had been drinking. "No, I have not been drinking any alcohol," my uncle replied. The missionary insisted several times, but my uncle still refused to admit. Finally my uncle told the missionary that he just didn't understand black people. "This is the way we smell at this time of the year!" my uncle told the missionary. The missionary could no longer insist, so he went on his way.

There was always a great discussion after each evening meal. We learned a lot of things regarding the dynamics between missionaries and Africans during the early years of missionary life in the Kajiji region. Two to three months later, this pastor talked about us in his church. He shared in his sermon that even pastors' children question church teachings on important issues such as the use of alcohol by church members. After I learned about what this pastor did, I started to question the sincerity of church leaders and wondered where in the world one discussed hard questions and issues of life if not in the family or the church. What right did he have to make public our family discussion? I began to wonder if pastors could be trusted with confidential information.

For several months, I also shared a bed with a young man who attended junior high in Kajiji. He came from a village about a day's walk away. I didn't know exactly what his relationship was to our family, but he called my parents his grandparents. Many people did, so it didn't make any difference anyway. We accepted him as a family member. His contribution included doing dishes, carrying water, and, from time to time, ironing clothes for my parents, as we all did.

As kids, we played very hard each day. After school and after finishing our chores at home, we either went to play soccer or to hunt for birds. We were very tired by the time we came back home in the evening. As a result, I slept very deeply during the night.

Over time, I began to suspect that my older bedmate was sexually abusing me in some way while I slept. I finally started to fear the night and was scared that something was going to happen to me soon. So I decided to pay attention and sleep lightly for several nights. One night as I lay in my bed half awake, I felt this young man start trying to molest me again. I coughed, and then got up from the bed. Right away, he knew that I was aware of what had been going on. I told him that I was going to tell Mom and Dad in the morning. He was scared and asked me to keep it secret between the two of us. I refused and told him my parents trusted me and that he wasn't going to get out of this one. I told him that if he kept insisting, I would wake up my parents that night instead of waiting until morning.

The next day, I told my mother about what I had experienced during the night and over the past several months. I chose not to tell my brother Tshinabu, who was home from boarding school, or my two cousins living with us then. I knew that if I did, they would beat up the young man and ask my parents to kick him out.

My mother listened very carefully as I told her the story. She was angry and wondered why I had not told her earlier.

She promised to talk it over with Dad that morning. They discussed it and decided to confront the young man. He admitted his wrongdoing, and my parents told him that he would be forgiven, but that he must promise never to repeat his actions.

It was total forgiveness because my parents didn't kick him out of the house. They found a single bed for him and never again had him share a bed with anyone else. I told the other two kids who were in the room with us what happened. We agreed to watch out for each other and inform my parents if this young man ever repeated his bad behavior. He never did.

I saw him several years later after he had left our house. He was married with several children. He had gone to a Bible school and was a pastor in a church in a remote village more than 90 miles from Kajiji. He is no longer living, however. I have always wondered if he ever repeated his act of sexual misconduct toward children.

I was innocent and naïve then. I didn't know anything about child molestation. My parents handled it in a way that provided me protection. I felt safe and didn't have to dwell on it during my adult life. I just could not understand why he wanted to have sex with innocent boys.

In college, I learned more about sexual abuse of children, and I felt sorry for this man. I was grateful for the way my parents dealt with him. Confronting this young man on my behalf was a sign to me that they loved me and would never let anyone harm me. Furthermore, it was a confirmation that I was never alone in any situation I might find myself in.

~

I guess I have always been an alien without realizing it. I never thought much about it as a child. I always knew that I was Chokwe and Congolese and that was all there was to it.

Then I was granted an American green card after Linda and I got married in 1984. This afforded me the privilege of entering and leaving the United States without a visa. I could also work and pay my taxes to Uncle Sam. One day while entering Canada at the Winnipeg airport, an immigration officer asked me where I was from and I told him that the passport in his hand was from Congo.

He told me that I needed a visa to enter Canada. I answered him by indicating that I had a U.S. residency status. I showed him the green card. He looked at it then he said, "Oh, you are an alien." I told him that I wasn't one. He insisted that I was. Finally I told him I was visiting Mennonites in the Winnipeg area who are part of my family and that I was speaking at a conference where the topic was "We Are Not Aliens." He laughed, stamped my passport, and let me go.

With most of my family being in Congo, I never considered myself an alien. Then I discovered that my dad's family had relocated to Congo from northern Angola when my dad was almost 12 years old. His brothers and several cousins moved to Shambungu, where the missionaries had established a mission station. This proximity made them among the first young people to be reached by missionaries. The missionaries brought them to the station, where they received basic training in reading, writing, and math. In addition, they learned Bible verses. Those who excelled in their studies were sent to other villages to teach other young people. If you were trustworthy, you got a job working in a missionary's home as a house boy or taking care of a missionary's garden.

Sometimes a young man might start working in the garden or taking care of livestock for the missionaries. Then, with time, he moved inside the house, first to do dishes under the supervision of the missionary's wife, who later might teach him how to make white people's food. As an adult, I noticed that before current Bible and theological schools were established, almost all the African pastors working in MB mission stations had worked either as cooks or gardeners for missionaries. I guess if you knew how to take care of a missionary, his family, and their animals and they all survived, you could be trusted to take care of people of God who are assigned to your care.

My dad became one of those trustworthy young people, starting with missionaries working under the group Unevangelized Tribal Mission, then later with missionaries from MB Mission and Service. I think my dad did everything that local people were allowed to do. He was sent to several villages as a teacher. After he and my mother were married, they played the role of house parents for young girls who were brought from their villages to attend school. He also worked as a house boy for one of the missionary families. When I think of our family time together following meals in the evening, the best moments were when dad told us stories about working as a house boy.

Missionaries were very strict in the way they dealt with local people. I think they needed to teach them discipline. At noon, my dad and the other workers were required to stay away from the house because missionaries needed to take their midday rest. You had no reason to wake them up unless it was a serious emergency. They were responsible to make sure that no one walked near the missionaries' house or made noise when the missionaries were sleeping.

Cooking was a major endeavor for those working for the missionaries. Starting a fire in the morning was a challenge because the workers used wood stoves. They were taught how to check when the fire must be started in the morning so that breakfast could be prepared on time. Dad remembered one morning when the cook was behind schedule. The missionary walked into the kitchen and noticed the fire wasn't ready yet. He called the cook to come quickly into the kitchen. This poor man tried to explain, but the missionary wouldn't listen. He took the man's head and started rubbing it on top of the stove, which fortunately wasn't very hot yet. He told him never to be late again.

"Why didn't he accuse him to the local authorities?" we once asked my father.

"You just didn't do that during that time" was his answer. How could you anyway? Even government leaders of the time wouldn't listen to you when your problems had to do with white people. Furthermore, the missionaries were the ones who had taken you from your village. They had provided you an education and now a job. You somehow owed it to them to be a good servant.

Another of my favorite stories was about when my father was a junior member of the houseboy team for one of the missionaries. The whole time he worked inside the missionary's house, he didn't run into any major problem. But he recalled one act of mischief that the missionary could not punish him for.

For some time, my father had noticed that just about every day after his nap, this missionary always screamed at his workers. Dad started to observe him for several weeks and noticed a pattern. After his nap, the missionary went to a cupboard and poured something into a glass. He drank it, then put the glass back behind the dishes. One day my father tasted what was in the bottle. It was alcohol.

The next day, the missionary called in all the workers and asked them if someone had touched a bottle in the back of the cupboard. Of course, no one admitted any wrongdoing. My father was the only person who knew, but he never said a word. A day later, my father went to check again to find the bottle was gone. The missionary couldn't believe that no one had actually touched his bottle, so he limited access to a certain part of the house for all the people working for him except for my dad. If this missionary had only known.

Dad's work as a houseboy earned him enough respect that later, he and my mom became house parents for some girls

The author's father, Isaac, left, leading a communion service in Kajiji, Congo.

from a distant village. He also was a station driver and station manager and finally was ordained as a pastor.

My father was also a stubborn man. He wouldn't take "no" for an answer and he wouldn't let people push him around. I think he did a good job of passing on that character trait to me. He wasn't afraid of anyone, whether they were military, government officials, or missionaries. I remember when my dad once took the mission station vehicle with a group of other church leaders to several villages for evangelism and baptism services. He had hoped to return early Sunday afternoon, but for some reason he was delayed. I remember a big crowd outside our house that day. It was the practice in Kajiji that, after a trip, people came to greet those returning from wherever it was. For us kids, Dad coming back from a trip also meant the possibility of him bringing back some goodies or meat from the villages he had visited. One of the senior missionaries also came to our house that afternoon.

"Why are you so late, Pastor? You promised to come back early in the afternoon," this missionary said to my father, without even saying "hello." My father continued to unload the vehicle as if he had not heard a word. "Did you hear me?" the missionary shouted. Dad continued for a few more minutes, then turned to the missionary and told him to go home and said he would bring him the key for the vehicle later. Then he added, "I know this is your vehicle because it was purchased with money from your people. However, just because it is your money that purchased it does not earn you the right to be disrespectful and lack courtesy towards other people." The missionary left without saying another word. I don't know what they talked about later when my father finally went to drop off the key, but he stayed much longer than usual before coming home.

CHAPTER 12

What Is Home?

1950s–1970s

For a long time, if someone asked me where my home was, the answer was simple: Kajiji. Then I discovered my roots go back to Angola. I also lived in Kikwit, 285 miles from my birthplace, then in Kinshasa, 620 miles away. Now my bed and dining table are in Fresno, California. So where is my home?

As a child, I was told that home is where your umbilical cord was buried. I guess that must be Kajiji then. But why do I always have this uneasy feeling of being a foreigner no matter where I live? Why am I losing that sense of home about Kajiji? I guess for my own sense of security, I still claim Kajiji as my home, or at least as my home of origin. I also am married to an American by birth who is a daughter of an immigrant father. Since 1999, we have lived in Fresno. Does that make Fresno my home just because it is where I pay my mortgage and taxes?

Kajiji is a beautiful little village built on the edge of a high plateau 3,000 feet above sea level and overlooking the Angolan border in the Bandundu province in Congo. In some ways, one could consider Kajiji an artificial milieu. It is neither a typical Congolese village nor an urban modern town. Kajiji was established by missionaries of the Unevangelized Tribal Mission in 1940. This mission station was initially established at Shambungu, about 30 miles from its current location. My dad told us the missionaries moved the station to its current spot because one of them had died of malaria in the older location. Furthermore, according to my father, the missionaries wanted to reach out to villages located in the valley of the Lunda Plateau.

Kajiji's beautiful climate and view feels like paradise on Earth. The climate in Kajiji is so pleasant that when I was in high school in Kikwit, we considered going back home after nine months away as going back to the "cold country." The summer months, from mid-May through mid-August, are usually cool and sometimes even very cold. Although all of us kids in Kajiji had never been in Europe, we considered Kajiji to be like Switzerland. For outsiders, arriving in Kajiji was like reaching the end of the world because all the roads seemed to end there. However, for some of us who were born there, Kajiji was just the beginning of our world.

Life in Kajiji was built around church-related activities—a hospital with 150 beds serving an area with about 150,000 people, a primary school, a nursing school, and two high schools, one of which trained girls in home economics. Each child born in Kajiji dreamed of becoming a teacher, nurse, pastor, or village evangelist. Not far from the mission station was a government post. People who worked in government jobs were perceived as less than trustworthy. As a result, no one wanted to be like them. Going into business also wasn't an option. The only businesspeople around were Portuguese. The three Congolese merchants I knew, including one of my uncles, lived some distance from the station. Each had left the station because they had decided to marry more than one wife.

Being a physician seemed out of reach because all the doctors working at the Kajiji hospital were white and from North America. The only Congolese doctors we heard of were from the big cities, but we never saw one in Kajiji. As a child, I heard a lot of myths about European-style medicine. Some people in the villages told stories about how these doctors were seen visiting cemeteries at night, especially on the eve of operating days. Some believed the white doctors did this to ask their ancestors how to do successful operations. Villagers sometimes wondered how these white doctors could open someone's stomach and remove harmful tissue, even while the patient survived. Only white men could do this, some of them thought.

Another myth was about the incineration of soiled materials at the hospital. I learned about this rumor several years later when I was working as both the hospital administrator in Kajiji and as the national coordinator for the public health program. An elderly lady asked me during one of my maternal and child health clinics in a village 45 minutes from Kajiji if our census had gone down in the hospital. I asked her why she thought this had happened. She told me that people had the impression that we do more incinerating at the hospital when our census starts going down. They believed that when we incinerated, the smoke attracted more patients to the hospital.

With its hospital and schools, Kajiji was meant to bring together people of different tribal and ethnic backgrounds. The two main tribal groups, Lunda and Chokwe, have cohabited for many years. They both were part of the Lunda Kingdom and the Bantu people.

Lunda and Chokwe were very involved in the slave trade, especially on the Angolan side of the kingdom. During that period, the Portuguese had hoped to deal directly with the Lunda for slaves and thus bypass the representatives of the other kingdoms that acted as intermediaries. Apparently entertaining similar ideas, the Lunda attacked these kingdoms in the 1760s. The Lunda, however, proved no more successful than the Portuguese at totally subduing these kingdoms.

Tensions between the Chokwe and Lunda in Kajiji occasionally flared into an active war. During the Congo rebellion of the 1960s, Kajiji wasn't affected directly by the conflict. However, the rebellion revealed the impact of the standoff between the two tribes. Although we were far from affected areas, when armed conflict started to spread in the Bandundu Province, the missionaries were evacuated to Kinshasa.

One day when I was about 15, more than half of Kajiji's inhabitants fled to neighboring villages. There were only a few families left in Kajiji in addition to hospital patients and their helpers, and a few dozen out-of-town students attending the nursing school. My family didn't have a choice but to stay. My father was the senior pastor as well as the mission station manager. He had promised the missionaries that he would guard their homes and goods while they were away. I remember when they brought him the keys to all the houses, one of the missionaries told my father to release the key to rebels or soldiers if it meant making a choice between material goods and the lives of our family members. Twice a day, my father made rounds to all the houses to make sure everything was intact. Many times he took me with him.

One early morning, soon after the daily prayer time held around 6:30 a.m., a friend of my dad told him he had heard that a truck full of soldiers was seen heading for Kajiji from a military base in Kahemba. He told my dad to be careful and to send his family away that day. My dad came back home around 7:30 a.m. to tell us to stay home, but my mother was committed to going to her field with two other women whose families had stayed. Soon after lunch, as he did every day, my father went to visit and pray with patients in the hospital. About 1 p.m., a truck full of soldiers arrived in Kajiji. While the truck was still moving, the soldiers jumped out and dispersed around the mission station.

"Where are Ngana Jacques and Muhunga Celestin?" they asked. Ngana Jacques was my maternal uncle and a nurse at the hospital. When the missionaries left, he and another nurse were left to run the hospital and the dispensary. Muhunga Celestin was a teacher, and his village was just a couple of miles away from Kajiji. Both were Chokwe. Both

Uncle Jacques and Celestin practically grew up in our home. Muhunga Celestin was like a big brother to my siblings and me while he was going to school in Kajiji. I understood he was related to us on my dad's side of the family.

My father was still at the hospital when a large group of soldiers invaded the hospital grounds. My father introduced himself to the soldiers, then was asked to move toward the front of the hospital together with all the nurses and nursing students. While everybody was gathered in one place and encircled by soldiers, they started questioning my dad about the two men's whereabouts. He told them he had not seen them since the early morning prayer meeting in church. They threatened to kill him if he wouldn't tell the truth. He repeated that he had not seen them since prayer time.

One of the soldiers told my dad that they were planning to take all the girls in the village with them. "You will kill me first before you touch any of these kids who were entrusted to me by their churches and parents when they came to study or work in Kajiji," my father replied.

One soldier moved in front of my father and put his machine gun to his head, while another soldier kicked him very hard in his right shoulder, knocking my father to the ground. The soldiers told him to stay on the ground, but my father started rising and raised his right hand toward heaven and prayed out loud, "God, forgive them for all their wrongdoings. I pray for you to take my life if that is your will."

A soldier who looked like an officer and the leader of the group, after seeing my father fall on the ground and pray, gave him a hand and invited him to get up. "You know this is not why we came here," the soldier told the others while holding my dad's hand. He asked my dad to sit close to him, then began to inform him about what was going on.

The soldiers had been sent to pick up two cows from a farm near Kajiji. When they arrived at the government post, they discovered a plot to arrest Uncle Jacques and Celestin.

It was a tribal-motivated plot, devised by a Lunda who was head of the government post. He could not include my dad in the plot because the government leader had married into my extended family. The soldiers didn't know about that relationship when they hassled my dad.

Celestin already had left Kajiji when the soldiers arrived. Uncle Jacques was on his way toward the hospital when he met a soldier along the path who was an old friend. The soldier informed him about the plot, and Uncle Jacques escaped without anyone noticing him.

The soldiers dismissed all the students, nurses, and my dad, but arrested a gentleman named Albert who was Uncle Jacques' brother-in-law. They told everyone that Mr. Albert would be taken to the military base until Uncle Jacques turned himself in. They didn't just arrest Mr. Albert, but a dozen soldiers kicked, beat, and pushed him before binding his hands and feet. They asked him to get into the truck by himself. Because he couldn't, they continued beating him with their rifle butts. By the time the soldiers had left, his whole face was swollen beyond recognition, and he was bleeding from his mouth, nose, and ears.

The soldiers picked up the cows they had come for, firing three shots to kill them before loading them on their truck. Because Kajiji was at the edge of the valley, the gunshots were heard in many surrounding villages. Word spread that day that the Chokwe reign in Kajiji was over because Uncle Jacques, Celestin, and my dad were now dead. Following this episode, I realized that maybe I had been naïve about the tribal conflicts around me. But this was my hometown, and sometimes, it was filled with conflict and danger.

CHAPTER 13

In Search of a Professional Home

Mid-1960s–1970s

My flight between Washington, D.C., and New York one winter day in 2004 was delayed because of bad weather at Dulles International Airport. We had already left the gate at Dulles, so we just sat waiting in the aircraft for the situation to clear up.

My seat neighbor offered me a magazine and asked where I was from.

"I live in Fresno, California," I answered.

He seemed puzzled by my answer, and asked, "Where are you originally from?"

After I told him about being from Congo, he asked me what I did for a living and how in the world I ended up in Fresno. "It's a long story," I told him. "I have a job that is not always easy to describe to most people I meet. My training is in public health, but I'm spending most of my time doing non-public health work. I think it goes back to my search for a professional home and my desire to serve those who have been marginalized in their societies."

That conversation reminds me that my life really is lived out of a suitcase. I have never had a job where I worked from 8 to 5. Preparing for my professional life has been a journey in itself. It took me from Kajiji to Kikwit via Fresno and Loma Linda. Each step of the way shaped my commitment to serving others, as well as informed my views on social issues.

Exterior of the Kajiji hospital in 2005.

As a child, I liked working with my hands. Although my dad was a minister, he worked building schools and churches. He worked as a houseparent, driver, and mission station manager. Doing multiple tasks wasn't a new concept for me. My first love and dream was to be a mechanic and a big truck driver. I was always fascinated by the smell of diesel, gas, and oil, and by the overalls that mechanics wore. I didn't just want to learn to drive, but I wanted to go for formal and academic training. Mennonites had schools that only offered training either in science or education. The only schools that provided higher-level training were Catholic or were managed by the government.

My father used to keep me occupied with work every summer I was home. I helped him paint houses and haul rocks, gravel, and sand in a small pickup. He taught me how to drive while I was in junior high, so I could help with small construction projects. With me driving, it was easy to get the other young people to lend their hands.

One summer, Katie Penner, one of the Canadian nurses at the Kajiji hospital, asked me to help her with some work in the hospital laboratory. I agreed. It was wonderful because it provided money for returning to school in the fall. The lab work wasn't the greatest, but I started to learn about taking stool and blood samples. She taught me how to do simple tests using a microscope.

One day, Katie asked me to assist her in the small operating room where she was changing the dressing of a man who had serious burns all over his body. The room smelled like a rotting animal. A couple of nurses had helped Katie bring in the patient. She gave me a pair of gloves to wear and asked me to help clean the man's arms, chest, back, and legs. I felt like vomiting, but I held my breath. From time to time, she asked me to turn the man over or to hold up his leg or arm while she carefully cleaned away dead skin and replaced dressings. I watched how she worked with such compassion and total attention to this man and his needs.

That evening, I continued to contemplate the idea of going to nursing school. I wanted to be like Katie. I guess my desire to work with oil and smelly diesel fuel transforming into to a desire to help wounded people. I never shared the idea with anyone, so when summer vacation was over, I went back to school in Kikwit. But the idea stayed with me, because the following summer I returned to work at the hospital. This time I worked with Sarah Peters, another Canadian nurse. I worked in reception and assisted with administrative work for the nursing school. When I left home for my last year of high in school in the fall of 1971, I decided that nursing wasn't for me. If anything, I thought I should try becoming a doctor.

Once I had ruled out nursing, I realized that I wanted to be like the American and Canadian physicians working at the Kajiji hospital. I wanted to be a surgeon. The mystery related to being a surgeon lured me—being able to open a person's body to repair it.

I left Kajiji in September 1971 for my final year of high school in Kikwit. While there, I learned about another professional opportunity. A team of Belgian and Congolese air force pilots visited Kikwit to recruit young people for service. They were looking for intelligent and physically fit young people. I was in good shape because I played sports and was among the top students in my class, so I figured this would be a great opportunity professionally. Besides, they were so well dressed in their air force uniforms that this alone was tempting. I picked up the enlistment forms and started filling them out. Before I had a chance to return them, however, my conscience struck me.

The author as a high school student in Kikwit in 1971.

Since childhood, I had been taught that I was from a peace-believing church. If I joined the air force, my profession would be to kill others. How was I going to explain this to my parents? If I sneaked out and enlisted without my parents knowing, would I be able to live with myself? The idea of killing became very ugly. I walked back to my dorm and never told anyone about that experience.

During my last year of high school, I was invited to live with a family in Kikwit. The husband was a truck driver for the church. In the fall, he went around the countryside to pick up all the students from MB mission stations and took them to Kikwit, where we had our church-run high school. At the beginning of summer, he drove all the students back to their home villages. He usually stayed with my family each time he drove to Kajiji. The summer before my last year of school, when he brought supplies for the hospital and the missionaries, he asked my parents if I could live with his family. My parents didn't object so I moved in with them in September 1971.

School was a half-hour walk from my new home. Walking to school was fun because several of us from the neighborhood attended the MB high school and walked together. We often left home at 6:30 a.m. in order to arrive by the time school started at 7:30. A friend of mine, Jocelyn, lived just a few houses down. She stopped by and we walked together. Our friendship made some of her classmates jealous. At the end of the day, she usually waited for the end of my soccer or volleyball practices so we could walk home together as well.

Just before Christmas vacation that year, I started experiencing severe headaches. Several trips to our small clinic didn't reveal anything. I was taken to the general hospital in Kikwit for further lab work, but it was inconclusive. The doctor prescribed malaria medicine, but my headaches persisted. I couldn't concentrate or study. Unfortunately, the headaches forced me to quit sports. The pain became excruciating, but nothing the doctors did helped.

The church had a large hospital at Pay Kongila, a couple of hours away from Kikwit, where my brother Tshinabu was working as a teacher in one of the MB junior highs. It was decided that I should go to that hospital for a systematic checkup. I was hospitalized for a couple of weeks and the headaches became less frequent. I returned to Kikwit and went back to school again. A month later, the headaches started again. My dad came to Kikwit for meetings and one day several of the church leaders prayed for me. Before they left, they anointed me with oil.

While my dad was in Kikwit, he decided I should go to Kinshasa for more tests, where I was diagnosed with cerebral malaria, a very dangerous strain that can kill or permanently debilitate the victim. The doctors prescribed strong malaria medicine and my health improved dramatically. However, the doctor said I should stop school for the remainder of the year so I could rest. Dad and I soon returned to Kajiji, which wasn't easy. I had dreams of finishing high school, but now I was forced to stay home. I couldn't do much reading either. My eyes became very teary each time I tried.

Sarah Peters, Arlen Gerdes, Helen Toews, and Elsie Fischer were among the missionary nurses at the Kajiji hospital when I returned home. They asked me if I was interested in teaching French at the nursing school, as well as helping with accounting and reception at the hospital. I didn't have anything to do

The author, center, spiking a volleyball in high school in 1971.

anyway, so during the daytime I worked at the hospital and in late afternoon, started practicing volleyball again. Teaching French and renewing my involvement in sports became very comforting and lifegiving.

Bob Buhr, a Canadian doctor, came to work in Kajiji that year with his wife, Jane. They were both very young, and before long we became good friends. I was interested in practicing English, and he wanted to improve his French. We agreed that Bob and I would meet on a weekly basis for a Bible study. I brought my New Testament in modern English, and he brought his French Bible.

We talked about life in Kajiji and the future of the hospital and schools if someday all the missionaries left. This was actually a serious concern. The church had encouraged many young people to study education, and many had become teachers and nurses. Each time there was trouble in the country and missionary doctors had to leave, the hospital had suffered, although the work had continued with the nursing staff.

One day, coming back from a village where we had taken a group of high school and nursing students for a church service, we started talking about the future of the Kajiji hospital. We both were sweaty and tired as we climbed the hills of the Kambululu River. After a few minutes of silence, Bob asked me if I ever thought about becoming a physician. I told him that my first passion had been to be a mechanic, but that medicine had crossed my mind from time to time. I said my family had seen the impact on the hospital each time the missionaries had to leave due to turmoil in the country.

I admitted that one barrier to my becoming a doctor was finances. Pastors didn't get paid much, and I told him how I once had requested a scholarship from the missionaries to study auto mechanics, but was turned down because it wasn't for theological studies. I said I really didn't feel called to be a pastor.

Bob asked me if I would be ready to go to medical school if I had someone to sponsor me financially. When I agreed, he said he would consider assisting me financially if I promised to come back and work at the Kajiji hospital. We walked back to Kajiji and continued our weekly Bible studies until the end of the summer.

Early in September 1972, I went back to retake my final year of high school with a new vision and perspective for my professional future. That same year, two cousins, Matshifi and Kasambashi, were accepted into medical school in Kinshasa. They paved the way for me. Now I wanted to be not only like the Canadian doctors—Bob Buhr, Ernie Schmidt, Rudy Hamm, and Ferd Pauls—but also like my cousins. If they could do it, I thought I could, too.

CHAPTER 14

Entering Fresno Pacific

1970s

In the early 1970s, all Congolese high school seniors were required to take a baccalaureate test administered by the state. Only those who passed could attend university. The tests were given on the same dates throughout the country. The results were then published in a special edition of one of the national newspapers. The year I finished high school, the test results were published late in August. The academic year at the university started each year on October 15. With test results being announced so late, few of us living far from Kinshasa could hope to enroll that same year, assuming we passed. Usually, the only chance of that was to have someone in Kinshasa, who was either a university professor or a student, pick up the application and make all the enrollment arrangements for you ahead of time.

An old friend in Kinshasa offered to assist me with the application process. He sent me the forms by way of Mission Aviation Fellowship, and two weeks later the MAF plane returned to bring mail and pick up passengers for Kinshasa. It gave me an excellent opportunity to send back all the forms and the required supporting papers. My chances of acceptance were very slim, but I gave it a try. I figured I had good test results, with high scores in the science section, and that this should help me attain my goal, even if my application came late in the selection process.

Meanwhile, Elsie Fischer asked me if I ever thought about considering studying in the United States. I wouldn't even think about it. My brother, Tshinabu, had just gone to study in France with assistance from the church. There was no way I would be considered for any financial assistance from the church to go study in the United States. After all, I was thinking about studying medicine and not theology. Elsie insisted I give it a try, not with church support but with help from private individuals. She informed me about two schools—Fresno Pacific College in California and Tabor College in Hillsboro, Kansas. She sent letters to both schools requesting application forms. To my surprise, I received the forms in a very short time. Bob, Elsie, Arlen, and Sarah helped me fill out the forms, which we then sent back via MAF to Kinshasa. One of the MB missionaries in Kinshasa mailed the forms to the United States.

Early in September 1973, I received a couple of letters from the two U.S. colleges I had applied to. I was accepted by Fresno Pacific in the premed program but rejected by Tabor. Then early in October, I received a second letter from Tabor indicating they had reconsidered my application and decided to accept me in the premed program. I discussed the two options with some of the missionaries in Kajiji to get an idea about which would be more suitable for me in terms of weather, culture, and connections with Africa. Fresno Pacific was very appealing and, after all, most of the movies I had watched about the United States had been from California and not Kansas. For many young people in Congo, going to California was like going to heaven on Earth.

Five missionaries in Kajiji agreed to sponsor me for medical studies in Congo or in the United States, pending my decision. Bob arranged for me to travel by MAF to Kinshasa with the option of either studying in Kinshasa, if accepted, or abroad if things didn't work out there. My brother, Mandjolo, was studying at the Kinshasa Theological School, which made life easy for me in the city. He showed me how to get to different offices I needed to visit. Sometimes he accompanied me when he didn't have classes or wasn't working at the MB bookstore. When he was very busy and I needed someone to accompany me, his wife, Maka, usually went with me. Maka knew the city very well, so I loved going downtown with her.

While in Kinshasa, I discovered that I was on a waiting list for medical school. The people in the admissions office asked me to return from time to time to check if my name had been selected. I thought my chances were good because I was at the top of the list. However, each time I went to check the list, someone told me to come back later. I was very discouraged after several trips to the admissions office. Bob came to Kinshasa for a meeting, and he suggested I pursue the Fresno Pacific option.

By mid-December, I had all the papers needed for going to Fresno except the visa. I needed to take an English proficiency test before they granted me a student visa at the U.S. consulate in Kinshasa. School was scheduled to start in January, and I had already missed the testing date. The next test was in March. I asked to meet someone at the consulate to explain my dilemma. The interviewer graciously welcomed me when I arrived. We started our conversation in French and, without my realizing it, the interviewer switched to English.

"Your English is very good, so why do you need that stupid test?" he told me. "I'll grant you the visa. If the college wants you to take the test, then let them give it to you while you are already in the U.S. Good luck to you." He asked me to pay at the front desk, then instructed me to pick up my passport the following day. By the end of December, I was on my way to Fresno.

I discovered before leaving Kinshasa that being on the waiting list for the university in Congo meant that I was actually accepted but needed to pay something under the table to get an official letter of acceptance. What did I know about paying something under the table? I grew up believing that you get what you deserve. You don't bribe people to get a service. Maybe I was naïve, but in this case I didn't mind.

I flew from Kinshasa to Los Angeles via Paris and London. I wasn't prepared for the cold winter in Europe. I remember arriving at Paris' Orly airport early in the morning. I had been dressed for tropical weather when I left Kinshasa. Upon arrival in Paris, I was ready to walk outside when the flight attendant asked me if I had a coat.

"It's very cold outside," she cautioned. Worse again, she told me I needed to go across town in a bus to catch my next flight to London before continuing to Los Angeles. I walked toward the door of the aircraft and felt a cold breeze blowing into my face. My whole body was cold and felt like I wasn't wearing any clothes at all. The flight attendant asked me to run to the terminal and offered to get me some coffee before I got on the bus for Roissy airport.

The building wasn't very far, but those few seconds of running felt like being dumped in a frozen lake. I wondered why no one prepared me for such a torture. I sat in the waiting room wondering what was next. While I was reflecting on my misery, the flight attendant brought me a nice, hot cup of coffee. I thanked her. She needed to leave, but she promised someone would help me board the bus. The room was warm and it felt so good drinking a hot cup of coffee.

In the airport, all I heard spoken was English. No more French, Lingala, or Kituba. I wondered if anyone would walk by speaking a language I knew. No luck.

The night flight between Los Angeles and Fresno wasn't long, but it seemed like an eternity. A gentleman sitting next to me asked me where I was from. "I'm from Congo," I answered him. "Where is that?" he responded. "It used to be Belgian Congo." I figured he at least knew where Congo was.

"Have you heard about Belgian Congo in Africa?" I asked him. "No, where is that?" he answered. I knew that I was lost after this answer. I wondered what kind of place I was going to where an intelligent looking person didn't even know where Belgian Congo was.

We landed in Fresno and the gentleman who didn't know where Congo was asked me if I knew where to get my luggage. He told me to follow him. The man was very friendly. We waited by the luggage carousel until my bag appeared. "Do you have anything else?" the gentleman asked me. "No, that's all. I only have this one piece," I answered.

"How about a ride to college? Is someone picking you up?" he asked.

"This is my first time in Fresno and I think someone from the college will pick me up, but I don't know who."

I could see this man was very concerned for me because he asked if I had any money in case I needed to make a phone call. I only had traveler's checks. He told me I needed dimes or quarters to make telephone calls. He waited with me to see if anyone was there to meet me. I gave him a couple of telephone numbers and he made some calls for me, but no one answered. Then I realized that these were school numbers and it was New Year's Eve. What was I thinking?

"I have to go, but I will give you these dimes to make phone calls if you need to," he said. Now what? I thought. Am I going to spend my first night in Fresno at the airport? But I didn't have to worry for long.

"Hi, are you Pakisa Tshimika from Congo?" a very tall man asked me. I was impressed. The man knew my name and pronounced it correctly. "Yes, I am," I answered with a sigh of relief.

"I'm Gary Nachtigall and I work at the college. I'll take you to the college campus and show you your room."

We drove to the Fresno Pacific campus and Gary took me to a building with two levels. We walked upstairs and he opened the door to one of the four rooms in the module, as he called it.

"Your roommate is Oni Ayodele from Nigeria," he said. "All the students are on vacation, but I think Oni is around and should be back sometime tonight. Welcome to Fresno Pacific College. Here is my home telephone number. Call me if you need anything."

He left and I fixed my bed and went to sleep. It was Friday night. That word of welcome was very comforting and reassuring. I'm not sure that either Gary or I realized how that first handshake sealed our friendship for many years to come.

Fresno Pacific became my home for the following four years. Life in the dorm was exciting. I learned about American culture through the young people I met in classes, in the dorms, and on the soccer field. Oni was very helpful, too. I remember one day while waiting in the cafeteria meal line, I asked Oni what they were serving for lunch. "Hot dogs," Oni told me.

"I think I'll go back to our room," I said.

"Why? It is good food," Oni insisted.

"We don't eat dog meat in my tribe, so I cannot imagine starting to eat it here," I replied.

Oni laughed and explained what hot dogs were. I knew the name in French but not in English. In fact, I had eaten hot dogs in Kajiji at Bob and Janice Buhr's home.

There were probably many other ways I discovered my naïveté while at Fresno Pacific. My first spring on campus shocked me. I was used to wearing uniforms in schools where girls were not allowed to wear shorts. Because Fresno Pacific was an MB school, I figured things there were the same, and that women dressed just as modestly, especially when playing sports. Wrong. As soon as the sun started shining, the girls started to wear clothes and shorts that would have had them kicked out of my school in Congo without much discussion.

One day during this first spring, as I was walking to our soccer field, I met three girls I knew from two of my classes. They were wearing only bikinis, and greeted me by name.

We walked together for a few yards, and then they put down their towels and laid on them to sunbathe. In the evening, I asked Oni if these girls didn't have the decency not to walk around the campus with such revealing outfits. I think Oni realized I was going through culture shock. He admitted he had gone through the same process himself when he first arrived in the United States. We discussed our different traditions and how they affect the way we view other cultures. I couldn't help but wonder why those missionaries who were my teachers didn't talk much about many of the general practices in their culture.

The next fall, I joined the soccer team. Oni and I were no longer roommates, but we saw each other often because we worked together on the maintenance team and played soccer together. One day I had just come out of class when Oni asked me if I wanted to join him for lunch in the cafeteria. We talked about the soccer game we had just played a couple of days earlier. Oni was one of the best defenders on the team. Oni and I laughed about one event during the game against a college from Southern California. We won the match, but during the game one of the players had hit me very hard and almost broke my leg. Next time the referee stopped the match, Oni looked that player straight in the eye and said, "If you hit my friend again, I'll break your leg." That player never got close to me for the remainder of the match. That event became a standard joke on the soccer team.

We had an excellent soccer coach, Ben Norton, who was a mentor, big brother, and adviser to all of us who were international students. As a Canadian who grew up as a missionary child in India, Ben could understand the issues of living in a foreign country. He became the glue that connected some of us foreign students on the team. Today, he is principal of a Christian school in Hong Kong, where he has hundreds of international students and teachers entrusted to his care.

I was not on a full scholarship when I was first accepted at Fresno Pacific. The college promised to cover my tuition after the first year if I kept my grades up. I also had a job on campus and my missionary friends back in Congo sent me some money. I studied hard that first year in spite of the language difficulty, and washed dishes in the school cafeteria. I also worked a campus maintenance job during the summer.

Working in a cafeteria at Fresno Pacific College in 1975.

I made enough money to cover my room and board and have enough left over to buy personal necessities. I did not need a lot of money to live on. Living away from my family while in high school in Kikwit taught me to be frugal. At Fresno, I bought most of my clothes at a nearby Kmart. I went to very few movies, but did enjoy Baskin Robbins ice cream when I could afford it. McDonald's became another favorite place to spend my pocket money.

Rather than buying a car, I bought a small motorcycle from the Heinrichs family, who eventually helped me purchase a larger model that I could take longer trips on.

As always, soccer was a passion for me. I had played it in high school and it was a pastime in Congo. We ate and breathed soccer, and our discussions on Mondays were always about the games played Saturday and Sunday. While in Kikwit in high school, I played in a small city league but dropped it to give priority to my studies. For me, playing soccer was for fun, and the competitive aspect was secondary. Maybe that's why I was surprised when people made a big deal when I scored three goals in one game at Fresno Pacific. While I had just enjoyed the game, I was told that I had broken the school record, which stood for many years.

As time went on, I realized that I wasn't the only naïve person on campus. I was asked once to speak to a freshman class about life in Congo. One student asked me if we had midwives where I grew up. He also wanted to know if children were born in hospitals.

"We didn't have midwife nurses where I grew up," I jokingly answered. "Actually, my mother was attended by a couple of female gorillas when I was born."

"Oh, really?" my naïve friend asked again. Several students in the class started laughing and he finally understood that I was just kidding. The same student asked me if we had cars in my country. With a serious look on my face I answered him, "We actually don't have cars in my country. We ride on different kinds of animals when we travel. However, there are a few white folks who have cars and they park them in the trees to prevent the natives from stealing them." I guess my cynicism was really coming through in that class, but all the other students understood the point I was making.

Attending a small college offered the advantage of close relationships with professors and staff. We had a mentor system. Several students had the same mentor and the group got together for few social activities during the year. That's how I saw my first professional baseball game. I soon realized my friends on campus were divided between being loyal to the Los Angeles Dodgers and the San Francisco Giants. My first game was in San Francisco. Baseball may be a kind of religion to some Americans, but all these years later, I still have not embraced it.

In 1986, I was selected to receive Fresno Pacific's Alumni of the Year award. I was humbled by the choice. Unfortunately, I was in Congo at the time, so I could not attend the presentation. Instead, my American parents, Wes and Ann Heinrichs, and my in-laws, John and Hulda Kroeker, accepted it on my behalf.

CHAPTER 15

Finding a New Dream

Mid-1970s–1980s

After my car accident, there were those who thought my career in surgical medicine was over. How can you operate on someone when your fingers are so crooked you can't even shake hands properly? I continued to think about this after I left the hospital following my accident and resumed my studies at Fresno Pacific. I was so close to my dream, and had been accepted to medical school in France, but now someone had to bathe, dress, and drive me everywhere.

I spent many hours with three of my science professors trying to figure out what my best professional options were. One day our genetics professor, Dave Pauls, took all of us from the science department to Stanford University in Palo Alto for a conference. I asked one of the professors at Stanford what the options were in the medical field for disabled people who still had a passion to serve. After some reflection, he suggested pathology or public health.

"Pathology—would I have to deal mainly with dead bodies?" I asked.

"Sometimes, but you can teach or work in a lab," he replied.

"How about public health? What will I do if I choose that option?" I asked.

He explained the different branches of public health—nutrition, health education, epidemiology, maternal and child health, biostatistics, and other fields. Most of the work in public health involved living people. That sounded more interesting than pathology. He suggested some of the well-known schools in the country that provide excellent training in public health.

"If you are interested in a school that has a church background as well as a good academic program, you might want to consider Loma Linda University," he said.

Loma Linda is supported by the Seventh-Day Adventist Church. When I had applied before to medical school, I sent letters to several universities in Europe because I wanted to study in an environment where tropical medicine was part of the curriculum. This time, I decided to apply only to one school. I told God that if I were not accepted, I would never try any other health-related professions. Soon, I applied to Loma Linda's School of Public Health.

In the meantime, the lack of physical activity was taking its toll on my body. Muscles atrophy, and some people get bed sores from lying down for a long time or sitting in a wheelchair. There were other difficulties as well.

One weekend, my roommate, Randy, had gone to play basketball, so I was in our apartment with a couple of friends, Laurie and Sharon. I began to experience pain in my lower abdomen. I also noticed blood in the urine-collection bag on my leg. I almost panicked. When Randy returned, I asked him to wheel me into the bedroom because I wanted to tell him what was going on.

At Fresno Community Hospital, a young doctor examined me and found nothing wrong. I lay on a bed in the emergency room in excruciating pain. I could hardly stand up. While they waited for lab results, the doctor ordered me some pain pills. Another hour passed before the doctor came back to my room and told me they couldn't determine what was wrong. They advised me to see my regular doctor on Monday.

The remaining part of the weekend was miserable. Early Monday morning, Randy suggested we call a urologist. The first question this doctor asked was whether the doctor in the emergency room had done any tests to rule out kidney stones. Randy told him he didn't. At his office, the urologist ordered an X-ray, which revealed four large kidney stones in my bladder. Surgery was scheduled, and I was admitted to Clovis Community Hospital, where four quarter-sized stones were removed.

While in the hospital, I asked my friend, Laurie, to check my mail.

"Pakisa, you have a letter from Loma Linda University," Laurie said on the phone. "Should I bring it to you this evening?"

But I couldn't wait to hear the news and asked Laurie to read me the letter right away. There was silence on the line for a moment, and then I could hear Laurie screaming with excitement.

"You have been accepted, Pakisa! You have been accepted at Loma Linda University!"

With this, I knew my desire to serve in a health profession was being reaffirmed. In the fall of 1978, I moved to Loma Linda, where my professional life was shaped by colleagues and professors who have since become friends and colleagues.

Loma Linda was a wonderful study environment for me. I started in the epidemiology program, where I met Dr. Richard Hart, who had returned from several years of work in Africa. His last assignment was in Tanzania, where he worked as adviser to the ministry of health. One day he asked me what I was studying.

"I don't think epidemiology is the right place for you if you want to go back to Africa," he counseled me.

He suggested I study international health, a new department at Loma Linda geared to training people interested in working outside North America. Soon, I requested a transfer and Dr. Hart assisted me in making the transition.

Loma Linda became my home from 1978 to 1980. I actually didn't know much about the Seventh-Day Adventist Church until I started attending classes there. A woman I knew only as Ms. Marshall, who helped find me a place to live, was the head of the occupational therapy department. She was disabled herself, so she understood my housing needs. As time passed, we became good friends and I usually stopped by her office just to tease her for a few minutes.

She introduced me to Donna, a Japanese woman who was teaching in the occupational therapy school. She was very kind and one day asked if I was doing any physical therapy since moving to Loma Linda. When I told her I wasn't, Donna asked Ms. Marshall if she could get me into a program at the medical center. Another therapist, Helen, was the wife of my biostatistics professor. She urged me to work hard, or teased that she would tell her husband I was a lazy bum.

I learned some other lessons, especially about Seventh-Day Adventist culture, the hard way. I met Jenny not long after I started school. She was from Australia. She introduced me to another student colleague, Carolyn, then to Scott and Annette. The university was conducting a series of conferences on marriage, divorce, and remarriage. All the students were required to attend the Friday evening meetings. After the session ended, my friends and I were standing in the fellowship hall. "Do you guys want to go out for coffee?" I asked my colleagues. There was total silence. "Don't you guys like coffee?" I continued. I thought it was odd that no one even responded.

"Can I talk with you for a second, Pakisa?" Carolyn finally said. "Coffee is not part of the culture here. Going out to a restaurant on Sabbath is not encouraged, either, and that is why no one said a word when you asked your question." If I had not been black, I am sure my face would have turned completely red from embarrassment. We all walked outside and decided to go to the house of another friend, Marie, for pie and other refreshments.

The two years working on my master's degree in public health at Loma Linda were very rich in new relationships and professional development. I enjoyed all the classes, especially those taught by Dr. Hart. He was such a wonderful teacher and had many years of experience in international health. Jenny and I played tricks on Dr. Hart from time to time, and he had such a good nature he took it very well.

One day he walked into the class in a suit and tie, but wearing tennis shoes. Jenny and I noticed it right away. "Is this a new style, Dr. Hart?" I asked. Our other classmates didn't understand why I had asked the question, but Jenny started laughing and Dr. Hart got the joke right away. He smiled, then raised one foot, and the others in the class finally got it, too.

What made my Loma Linda experience especially good were my friendships with professors and fellow students, particularly Carolyn and Jenny. Carolyn was from Northern California. Her husband had a very stable job, so he could not move when Carolyn decided to go back to school. Every other weekend, Carolyn flew to Sacramento to be with her husband, while the other weekends, he came to Loma Linda. Our fun together was making carrot cake after a long day of study. Sometimes we called each other at 11 p.m., to go to the nearest store to pick up some carrots for baking a cake. By the time we finished it was close to 2 in the morning. More than 26 years later, we are still connected. Jenny is back in Australia and Carolyn in northern California, serving on the board of directors of a non-profit organization I established in 2003. Most recently, Dr. Hart has been at Loma Linda serving as provost.

In 1987, I went back to Loma Linda to work on my doctorate in public health. Dr. Hart had been appointed dean of the school of public health. Once again, I discovered wonderful professors: Dr. Hopp, who became the chair of my disserta-

The author with his wife, Linda, at Loma Linda University graduation in 1991, when he received his doctorate in public health.

tion committee; Dr. White, my academic adviser; and Dr. Johnston, head of the doctoral program. I always looked forward to my time with Dr. White. She had worked in Africa, so she understood my need for additional training. Actually, Dr. White became like a mother to me. She was a soft-spoken person who conveyed the feeling that she genuinely cared and was there for me.

My second period at Loma Linda, while I worked on my doctorate, was enriched by the fact that I was married. Linda had a job, but we made time to do lots of activities together. Camping became one of our favorite pastimes. Once, Linda chose a site for camping that she believed was along the beach by the Pacific Ocean. However, when we arrived that night, we discovered it was not only far from the beach but close to a busy railroad track. We joked about this for a long time and decided Linda wouldn't choose our campsites on her own anymore.

My working as a teaching assistant also provided a different kind of community for us. Several of my colleagues in the doctoral program made life very enjoyable for us. During the ceremony when I was granted my doctorate in public health, Dr. Hart almost choked when my name was called. He gave me a bear hug, and we both had tears in our eyes. He had counseled me to enter public health as a profession and had been my hero from the day I met him. I could not think of anyone better to hand me my diploma. Many of my American family and friends were there to see me graduate, as well as some Congolese friends from Southern California.

The next day, we decided to go to Disneyland to celebrate my achievement.

In 1995, I received the Alumni of the Year award during Loma Linda's commencement ceremony. That June, Linda, Sonja, and Norm accompanied me to accept the award from Dr. Hart. As I received the honor, I noticed the many flags from foreign countries that stood behind me on the platform. They were like a cloud of witnesses from around the world, testifying to the global nature of my calling.

CHAPTER 16

A Home Away from Home

1970s

Whenever someone moves far from home, homesickness is sure to set in. I first left home soon after junior high, so I knew how to take care of myself. When I went away to high school in Kikwit, I knew I would be gone for nine months, and that in July I would go home again to Kajiji.

However, I arrived in Fresno not knowing when, or how, I would go back home to Africa. Hardly any students were on campus the weekend I arrived because of the Christmas and New Year's break. I asked my roommate if there was a Mennonite church near the college. He told me about Butler Avenue MB Church, less than five minutes' walk from the campus. On Sunday morning, I walked there and found myself in a nice church. Being the only black person present that morning, I wondered if this place was right for me. I expected to find many black people in Mennonite churches. But here I was, my first Sunday in Fresno, and I was the only one.

At the end of the service, the pastor asked where I was from. I told him I had just arrived from Congo and was a member of an MB church there. Several people from the congregation also greeted me in the fellowship hall.

"Hi, we are Wes and Ann Heinrichs and we want to welcome you to our church," a man said from behind me as I was getting ready to leave. I introduced myself.

"Do you have plans for lunch?" Ann asked me.

"Not really," I said.

"Would you like to join us for lunch?" they asked. I accepted the invitation, and together with two other couples they took me to a restaurant at the airport. Everything seemed so new, and I was impressed that these people I didn't know would take me out to lunch.

"How do your spell your first name?" one of the women asked.

"P-a-k-i-s-a," I responded. I could see she was wondering how in the world she was going to remember it.

I saw Wes and Ann several times again after that initial visit. One day, the telephone rang and it was Ann.

"All of our kids are coming home for a Sunday meal," she said. "Would you like to join us if you are free? We would like to introduce you to our children." When I arrived for the meal, I saw a new face, Norm Wiens. I had seen Norm on campus. He was one of the few young white students who spent time playing with black kids from the neighborhood. I was impressed with him but had never talked with him before. He was married to one of the Heinrichses' daughters.

During the meal, Wes and Ann introduced me to their three daughters and their husbands—Kenny and Linda, Norm and Sonja, David and Dianna. "We have another daughter, but she is studying at Tabor College in Kansas," Ann said.

"Welcome to our family, and we want you to feel at home," Wes added.

I was impressed with this unusual family. Beside the fact that the four girls were adopted, they also were from different ethnic and racial backgrounds. Sonja, the first to be adopted, was Cherokee, Dutch, and Irish. Marcia, second in adoption, was a Native American of Umatilla and Nez Perce descent. The other two girls, Dianna and Linda, were German sisters. I think this mosaic of backgrounds also attracted me to the family and made me feel welcome. That meal sealed my relationship with their family. I knew that now I had a home away from home, just as my parents had assured me before leaving Congo that God would provide for me.

Weekends became bearable now that I had a family. My new parents invited me to family meals and on trips to Pismo Beach. Wes taught me how to use his lawnmower. Dianna began teaching me how to swim in the little pool her family had in their back yard. The first sessions were full of laughter. Whenever I jumped into the pool, I sank like a rock. We still laugh about these mishaps more than 30 years later.

Grandma Heinrichs (Wes' mother) and Grandpa Queen (Ann's father) were living with Wes and Ann when I met them. They were advanced in age and needed continuing care. Grandpa Queen was a self-taught veterinarian from a small town in Colorado. There were two groups of people he didn't care for, however—blacks and Democrats.

I remember coming home several times for short visits. I always found Grandpa Queen in a special chair that was set up for him. He had problems hearing, so they fixed a little speaker beside his left ear so he could follow the news every day.

"What's in the news?" I asked him one day.

Jimmy Carter had just been elected president, and Grandpa Queen couldn't understand it. In fact, it took him a long time before he accepted the result of the election.

Just like in my family in Congo, joining the Heinrichs family also meant sharing times of joy, pain, and sorrow. One morning in April 1976 I was driving to northern California to pick up my roommate and soccer teammate, Doug, who was riding my motorcycle, which had broken down. The sun was rising just as I passed the city of Merced. It looked so beautiful with white, red, and yellow colors that I decided to stop beside the freeway just to contemplate the beauty. It reminded me of the sunrise and sunset back in Congo. I had taken my camera with me, so I took several pictures of the sunrise. I picked up my roommate and then we drove back to Fresno.

That evening, I received the news that Sonja had given birth to a little girl, Heather. Her birth reminded me of the beautiful sunrise I had just experienced that morning. It was a gift from heaven. When I went to see baby Heather I was overwhelmed by a wonderful feeling of joy and excitement at this new life. I took my pictures to be developed that week and had one of the sunrise pictures enlarged and presented as a gift to Norm and Sonja for Heather. In the years that followed, Heather became a cherished niece. She is now married and I had the privilege of attending her wedding and praying at the reception that followed. Each time I see her, I remember that beautiful April morning.

Two years after celebrating Heather's birth, an accidental death struck the family, in February 1978. The telephone rang in my apartment at Fresno Pacific.

"Can you come home now?" Ann said. Their daughter Linda's son, Jason, had drowned in their swimming pool that day.

Jason was only four years old when he died. Jason and I had developed a special relationship. Each time he came to his grandparents' house and I was there, he usually found me helping out with household chores.

One day while I was in the hospital in 1976, Jason was visiting his grandparents. He saw that the whole back yard was torn apart where Wes had taken out a small swimming pool. "Look what Kisa did!" Jason disgustedly told Wes after seeing the destruction.

"But Kisa is in the hospital," Wes told him. I am not sure he was convinced, but Jason knew he had to trust his grandfather's explanation.

It wasn't until I was brought home in a wheelchair one Sunday for a family meal that Jason realized I was no longer the same. He sat on my lap for awhile and I saw he had many questions, but didn't know where to start.

Now Jason was gone and I could no longer tell him the whole story of what had happened and why my life was never going to be the same.

CHAPTER 17

Becoming an American

1995–2002

I became a U.S. citizen on March 11, 2002, six months after the terrorist attacks of September 11, 2001. I was 50 years old and had been living in the United States with a green card since 1986. Two friends told me different stories about the process of becoming an American citizen. For one, it took almost two years from the time she applied. The second friend had been waiting more than five years and was still trying. With these two perspectives in mind, I sent my application to the Immigration and Naturalization Service branch in southern California. In the meantime, I continued to travel using my Congolese passport and a U.S. alien resident card.

I wasn't sure how badly I really wanted to become a U.S. citizen. Many friends in Congo could not understand why I had waited so long to apply. After all, my wife was American, and my friends viewed the United States as the country of opportunity and freedom.

In 1997, one high-ranking officer at the consulate in Kinshasa asked me, "Why did you return to Congo under such harsh conditions, when so many people in this country, given the chance, would leave in no time at all?"

I didn't have to think much about his question. "I guess I'm still proud of being Congolese," I said. "I just dream of a day that we Congolese will get our act together and realize that the grass is not necessarily greener on the other side of the fence. If we clean our house and put our resources to good use, maybe we will not envy the U.S. and Europe."

My efforts to become a citizen went smoothly. I sent in my applications, underwent an FBI background check, took language and history tests, and one day received a formal letter inviting me to an official naturalization ceremony.

Two weeks before the ceremony, I started to wonder if I made the right decision to become a citizen, especially under the administration of President George W. Bush. I didn't care for his foreign policy, and his father had contributed to the misery of my people in Congo by collaborating with President Mobutu during the Cold War, when the senior Bush headed the Central Intelligence Agency. Mobutu was destroying the country, and yet the senior Bush still called Mobutu a friend of the American people.

Now, here I was getting ready to become his countryman under his son's administration. Worse yet, the son seemed more arrogant than the father. I had been watching his speeches since the terrorist attacks of 2001. It scared me to see him alienating the United States from the rest of the world. I wondered if I really wanted to be part of an "ugly American" society.

I shared my internal conflict with two men from church who had been big brothers to me, Dr. Roger Fast and Paul Quiring. Both encouraged me to become naturalized because, in many ways, it would help me become more of a world citizen, acting as an ambassador of the church.

We arrived at the Fresno Convention Center half an hour before the ceremony. Several friends and family members came to witness it. The room was full with rows of people lined up to return their green cards and receive packages of material prepared for the occasion. Being "physically challenged," I was asked not to join the line, but to follow a woman who took my green card and escorted me to a seat in the front row. Linda and my dozen or so other guests were seated nearby.

We waited more than an hour for the ceremony to start. My friends Sonja Heinrichs and Joan Fast sat near me. As we waited for the program to begin, each one encouraged me to think positively about the process I was about to go through. Someone announced the entrance of the federal judge, and we were told that from then until the end of the ceremony, the room had, in effect, become a courtroom. Everything was going fine until they introduced the guest speaker. He was a lawyer who was a naturalized citizen himself. The minute he opened his mouth I knew I was in trouble.

"This is a big day for all of you," he said. "You came to this great country in search of a better life. You will not find another country as powerful as this country."

I felt like walking out. This was what I had been afraid of from the start. I have a lot of respect for this country and its people, but I wasn't becoming a citizen because I was looking for a better life. He continued to tell us how proud we would be one day when our children came back home after serving in the military to defend the U.S. flag and what it stands for.

I still wanted to walk out but realized I then would be in the country illegally because I already had surrendered my green card, my official residency document. I thought of many examples of national pride the speaker could have used, but why war imagery? We all know that wars don't solve the world's problems, so why was he using combat as an example of the best way to serve this nation? I looked over at my family and friends. I saw that Linda and Sonja knew my pain. They told me later how they had wondered what was going on in my head as this lawyer continued to speak, using examples that they knew didn't sit well with me.

The judge was very brief. After asking all the participants to raise their right hands and repeat the prescribed text, he congratulated everyone on becoming American citizens, with all its privileges and obligations. All participants were asked to go back to the same window where they had surrendered their green cards to receive their naturalization certificates. Once again I was asked to wait. The same woman who escorted me when I arrived soon brought my citizenship papers, congratulated me, and left.

I walked over to where my family and friends were. Linda, Sonja, Joan Fast, Nate and Kristin Fast, Gary Nachtigall, Wes and Ann Heinrichs, Linda's mom, Hulda, my pastors Bill Braun and Mary Anne Isaak, and our daughters Annie and Patience were there. They all congratulated me with hugs and kisses. Those who were Americans welcomed me into U.S. citizenship.

"I guess I am really one of you now," I told them.

CHAPTER 18

Preparing to Return Home

1980

I finished my master's degree studies at Loma Linda University in 1980. Now equipped with a master's degree in public health, with an emphasis in international health and focusing on maternal and child health, I was ready to join the work force and to start making a living on my own. After consultation with friends and family, I decided to go back to Congo despite my physical limitations. The work I had agreed to do meant a lot of traveling in the villages around Kajiji, as well as long-distance trips to Kikwit and Kinshasa. I thought about the logistics of traveling in the villages with only primitive toilets and outdoor latrines, not to mention beds without mattresses. I imagined having to wake up in the middle of the night to go to the restroom and then having it start raining outside. I kept thinking about the fear of eating food that didn't agree with me and suffering from diarrhea with only crude bathroom facilities to accommodate me. I was apprehensive about my decision, but I knew it was the right thing to do.

To test my endurance and patience, while on my way home to Africa in May 1980, I decided to travel alone in Europe for a month.

Was I stupid traveling alone in my physical condition? I was barely walking with a cane at that time. What if I got sick? What if I were hit by a car while crossing a street? What if I could not find a place to sleep? I didn't make any hotel reservations, except for a guesthouse in London. I told myself to take it on faith and that I'd be fine.

I purchased a 30-day Eurail train pass and flew to London for a week to visit Dr. Morley, a well-known specialist in tropical pediatrics. My university friend, Jenny, and I used to have discussions about who would be the first to meet our favorite public health specialists, Dr. Morley and Dr. Jeliffe. Jenny was jealous when I told her I had written Dr. Morley asking to visit his center on my way to Congo. I promised her that I would have Dr. Morley sign a couple of his books and send them to her.

Dr. Morley wasn't in London when I arrived. He was lecturing in the United States. But his assistant told me he would return while I was still in London. For two days, while waiting for Dr. Morley's return, I visited London night and day. I visited historical sites such as the royal palaces, Big Ben, and Piccadilly Circus. I was most fascinated by the night life —people from all over the world in cafés and theaters, or just walking. I usually found a corner at a café and watched people, my favorite public pastime. I wondered about what made them tick, wear the kind of clothes they wore, or choose the coffee or beer they drank. Sometimes I wondered if a couple I saw walking around was married or just friends enjoying each other's company on the beautiful streets of London.

"Oh my, what have they done to you? What a pity!" Those were the first words Dr. Morley said after I introduced myself. It was my English that had startled him, not my physical condition. He was sad that I sounded so much like an American.

My time with him was wonderful. He shared with me the different books he had written. He gave me some as gifts and I purchased others for friends. He invited me to join him in reviewing a film he was working on to promote maternal and child health for developing countries. I had many questions to ask him, and we talked about the importance of immunization and nutrition education for the tropics and how they can impact a child later in life. He was helpful in giving me advice on the issues of advocacy in health care, especially on behalf of mothers and children. Two days with him and his colleagues at the beginning of my public health career was a gift that continues to impact my professional life.

Following my time in London, I flew to Paris, where I stayed for a week with my brother, Tshinabu, before embarking on my month of lone travel across the rest of the continent. I had secured visas for France and England before leaving California, but nothing else. I figured I would apply for visas for the other countries as I traveled. While in Paris, I was granted a Benelux visa, which covered Belgium, the Netherlands, and Luxembourg. That was good enough for me to get started, beginning in the Belgian capital.

I had two reasons to stop in Brussels. First, Dr. Roger Fast and his family were living there. He was studying French and tropical medicine before going to Congo to work at the Kajiji hospital, where I would develop a public health program for the region. Second, Brussels embodied the historical ties Belgium had with Congo.

When I arrived at Brussels' main train station, Roger was waiting for me. He took my backpack and we started walking toward the parking lot. I heard voices behind us speaking Lingala, one of the languages from Congo. As soon as I heard Lingala, I knew I was no longer in North America.

The Fasts had three children then. Ruth was the youngest and became my special friend during my time in Brussels. I was sleeping on a mattress the family had set on a floor. Each morning when I woke up, Ruth was sitting by my head, staring and watching me with a big smile. I never knew how long she had been watching, but she was there every morning, silently staring. After she noticed I was awake, she took off to find her parents. Those moments each morning became very special because later, when Ruth was grown, she and I spent several good years together, first in Kajiji and then when her family returned to North America.

The Fasts and I visited many places in Brussels. One of the most fascinating was the African Museum. I wanted to see how many historical items I could find from my Chokwe people. The masks and small household items related to the Chokwe culture interested me the most. As we explored, something very small caught my attention. It was a small toy car made from match boxes, and wheels made from beer bottle caps. I laughed as I remembered how I used to make such toys as a child. Interestingly enough, the little toy car was made by a child in Kahemba, about 50 miles from Kajiji.

"So people have to pay money to see these little toys we made and for which sometimes our parents spanked us because they thought we were wasting our time," I thought as others commented on the ingenuity of the African children.

Several years later, I remembered this when Linda and I were traveling and camping during a trip between California and Kansas. We stayed in a Navajo Indian reservation in Arizona and spent a day taking a guided tour of the Canyon DeChelly, full of beautiful rock drawings of all shapes and forms.

Soon after we arrived in Kansas, I started describing for Nancy, my sister-in-law, the beauty of this canyon and all the drawings on the walls and rocks. She started laughing and I asked her why.

"I'm just imagining these little kids writing on the walls and the parents spanking them for ruining the walls," she said. "And today people come from everywhere to contemplate them with so much appreciation."

Maybe that is the way modern graffiti will be seen several decades from now.

CHAPTER 19

Traveling in Europe

1980

Given the chance, people often are kind even to total strangers. During my traverse of Europe in 1980, I stayed for three days in a small hotel in the center of Rome. The first evening I was there, the hotel owner asked if I wanted to join him for a drink. I agreed and he offered me a little glass of vodka.

"Do you like it?" he asked me. I had never tasted vodka before and it was strong. Would I offend him if I told him I didn't like it?

"Do you want another glass?" he asked me.

"No, but if you have something milder, that would be good," I answered. He poured a glass of Italian red wine, and we talked about the city and what to see and what to avoid. He promised to assist me and made arrangements for my taxis each day. He seemed happy to see me every evening when I returned to the hotel.

Before I left the United States for Europe and then Africa, an official of the California Rehabilitation Department helped me get a ticket for my travels. The Heinrichs family gave me a monthlong Eurail pass, and so with less than $300 in my pocket I left Fresno, believing God would provide for the rest of my needs along the way.

In Paris, my brother, Tshinabu, gave me the names of people he knew in Switzerland, southern France, and the Netherlands. I spent many nights sleeping in the train as my journey progressed. On a few occasions I stayed in pensions, especially when I needed a place for a hot meal and shower.

Along the way, particularly in the Netherlands and Switzerland, I looked up a few strangers who had ethnic Mennonite names and stayed with some of them. Often, these new friends would leave a small gift of money in my backpack to help me along my way.

But my journey still was filled with challenges. The day before I left Rome for Sicily, I went to visit the Colosseum. I was walking toward the ancient amphitheater when I realized that my left shoe had become untied. I was walking with a cane so I could not bend down to tie it again. I could not walk, either, because my foot started to drag.

I decided to see if someone nearby would help me. I asked the first several people who walked by if they knew English. The answer was no. How about French? The answer was the same. They all said, *"solo Italiano,"* "only Italian."

After several tries, I changed my strategy. I showed the people my left foot, but they couldn't understand that way, either. Finally, I decided to focus on women with children because I thought they would be more perceptive of something like an untied shoe. I saw a woman with two young kids coming toward me and asked her if she knew English or French. She didn't. I pointed to my feet and she looked puzzled at first but then burst into laughter. She knelt down and tied my shoe. I thanked her and she smiled. Walking on, she waved once and disappeared into the crowd.

I met another woman as I began walking up what seemed like several thousand steps leading to the top of the Colosseum. She spoke English. She was coming down and asked if I needed help going up. "No," I told her. She insisted and told me there were a lot of steps to maneuver. I said I could make it because there was a railing to hold. She looked at me and said, "You must be a stubborn man," with which I agreed.

The Colosseum was breathtaking. My history teacher, Mary Toews, used to talk about it as if she had lived during the time of the Roman Empire. She had shown us pictures of it and now I, the little boy from Kajiji, was standing and sitting in this historic place. It felt like a holy moment.

~

Another feature of my trip to Europe was encountering people from various countries. In this, I had been influenced a great deal by my schoolteachers.

Some of my American high school instructors didn't like the French at all. They seemed to love the French language, but not the people this wonderful language represented. I asked one why she disliked the French.

"They show too much affection in public," she told me.

Showing too much affection in public? What was she thinking? I saw a lot of that on my college campus. Compared to how people dressed in our church schools in Africa, I thought these American college students walked around practically naked on campus. In spring, girls even wore bikinis on the campus lawn. My high school teacher also said the French were promiscuous and arrogant. But are they any more promiscuous and arrogant than Americans? I am not so sure anymore.

My three high school teachers from France were among my favorites. One of them, Mr. Brottes, was an engineer in France and taught us math. He told us that humans didn't eat corn in his country. Instead, corn was raised for feeding animals. However, he told us that Americans ate corn just like Africans. That didn't go over well with us because we enjoyed eating corn during the harvest season.

Later, during my second year of school in Kikwit, I saw the other side of Mr. Brottes, who by then had become a good friend. His wife was pregnant and went to Kajiji to have her baby. Well now, I thought, this couple had really become one of us. When they came back from Kajiji, a friend and I placed an ear of corn on his desk and waited in the back of the room. He took the ear of corn and started eating it—again, just like an African. We laughed and he realized who had left the corn for him. From then on, he asked us to get him some corn whenever we went to the market.

I saw Mr. Brottes and his wife during my journey through France. My brother took me to their house for dinner. Their son, Olivier, was married and working already. Mr. Brottes was laughing when his wife invited us to the table. When I took my place, he brought a dish full of sweet corn.

"Do you remember?" he asked me.

"Oh yes, how could I have ever forgotten?" I replied.

We enjoyed a wonderful meal together while reminiscing about our time in Kikwit during my high school years.

In France, I wanted to visit Lyon, a city that would have been my home during my medical training if my life had not changed so dramatically following my car accident. I also wanted to visit the Alps from the French side. I had read about the resort at Chamoney and what a beautiful little tourist and ski town it was. I arrived there early one morning. As soon as I got off the train, I asked a lady who assisted me with my backpack if she knew of a hotel where I could spend two nights.

"Did you make a reservation before coming here?" she asked me.

Reservation?

"No, I didn't," I said. "Was I supposed to?"

"It's hard to find a place without a reservation here, but let me help," she said. We walked to a small restaurant and she disappeared for awhile. She came back with a smile on her face and said, "You're lucky, sir. I found a place for you. Do you want me to accompany you there? It is not that far. I can carry your bag."

I accepted her offer and we walked to the small hotel, where I registered for two nights.

"I am Steph," she told me as we said goodbye. "Would you like to join me for breakfast tomorrow at the restaurant next door?" We agreed to meet at 8 the next morning.

It was cool in the mountains, even though it was summer. I walked around for awhile, then went to eat lunch. I visited little souvenir shops and purchased a few gifts to take with me back to Congo. I met people from all over Europe, North America, Asia, and Latin America. Some were traveling as families, while others were with tour groups. I saw people from all walks of life. As I stopped in another coffee shop, I decided I wanted to taste something from Africa and ordered a cup of coffee from Tanzania. As I sat in this coffee shop, watching people walk by, I realized I was the only black person. Here again, the only people I didn't meet were those from Africa. In some ways, I wasn't really surprised. I had not met many Africans who traveled just for pleasure. I met some in London, Brussels, and Paris, but they were all traveling for business.

I felt very tired by 5:30 p.m., so I decided to take a short nap before I went to supper. I woke up once around 7 p.m. and figured I could sleep for a couple more hours and then go have a sandwich in one of the shops. Next thing I knew, it was 7 a.m., and I had just enough time to get ready for my breakfast rendezvous.

I arrived just as Steph arrived, and offered to buy her breakfast.

"You don't have to pay for mine. I have money. I can pay," Steph said. I thought for awhile, then several images started to cross my mind. I remembered while in college, I sometimes offered quarters to several classmates in our laundry room if they were short of change. They usually wouldn't take them because they felt they were supposed to assist me and not the opposite. After all, I was from Africa and we were all supposed to be poor. Many times I offered to pay for meals and got the same answer.

"Why can't Europeans and Americans accept gifts from Africans, even if they think they have more financial and material goods than we do?" I wondered. I even thought how ironic it was that Europeans and American had become very rich on resources from Africa, and yet they wouldn't accept simple gifts or gestures from an African person.

I ordered a croissant, scrambled eggs, strawberry yogurt, orange juice, and a cappuccino. Steph listened carefully as I ordered my breakfast. I could tell she had something on her mind. "What is it?" I asked her.

"Nothing really," she replied. It turned out that Steph wanted to know how I learned to like croissants and yogurt, because they were not African dishes. I asked her if she knew that there were French people living in the African jungle. She laughed. I told her that I met several Europeans when I was in high school. They lived in the trees in Congo, I told her. They came down from time to time to teach Africans about the civilized ways of eating. One of them talked about eating croissants and yogurt. I told her they also purchased coffee from the Africans, then served it to the Africans as French coffee. She was very impressed with my stories and yet could not understand why I was laughing.

"You're lying to me," she exclaimed.

"No, I'm not. Didn't you study that in school?" I asked her. "OK, I am lying," I admitted. We then talked about Africa and the stereotypes she grew up with regarding other cultures.

As we talked over breakfast, we didn't seem to worry about time. After all, I didn't have any plans for that day and she was on vacation. I think I drank more coffee that day than I had for a long time. She asked if I would take a walk with her. We made a tour of the same shops I had visited the day before. We talked about her sister, Marie Claire, who lived in

Lyon. She offered to give me her sister's telephone number so I could call her when I arrived there.

"Of course, any assistance I can get is more than welcome," I told her. It was almost 5 p.m. when she walked me back to my hotel. I told her that I wanted to visit Basel, Zurich, and Geneva in Switzerland first before I visited Lyon. She gave me her sister's address and telephone number and insisted that I call Marie Claire a couple of days before I arrived in Lyon. It had been two sweet days and it was time to move on. We hugged and kissed goodbye. I left the next morning for Switzerland.

I arrived in Geneva on a warm June afternoon. Two things interested me in Geneva: the World Health Organization and the Medical Commission of the World Council of Churches. I had heard so much about these two organizations that I wanted to visit them myself.

I guess I looked lost at the train station because a young woman in her late 20s asked me if I needed assistance. Her name was Eva. She worked for a women's organization that helped visitors find lodging, and guided them to tourist attractions in the Geneva region. She asked me to follow her to an office not far from where I had left the train. I told her I wanted to visit WHO and WCC headquarters. I also wanted to visit anything of great historical interest.

She made a few telephone calls, then said she had made a reservation for a hotel, as well as arrangements with a couple of people at WHO and WCC. She offered to take me to the hotel. I registered and received a discount because of her organization. She asked before she left if I needed any other assistance.

"I don't think so," I told her.

"I'm a university student and am on vacation and have time after work," she said. "If you want, I can show you around."

"Sounds good," I responded.

The next day, I visited WHO headquarters. I was impressed by the library and bookstores. I kept thinking about all the hospitals and schools, including medical schools in Congo, without books or reference materials. I remembered primary and secondary school kids who had never been in a library. I dreamed of someday establishing school reference libraries in my home country. At WHO, I received many books as gifts, especially those related to primary health-care delivery for developing countries.

In the afternoon, I went to visit the WCC office. I was introduced to the medical commission staff, who informed me about the ways they work in different countries. I learned about their contact in Congo at the Church of Christ of Congo in Kinshasa. They encouraged me to contact them as soon as I got back to Congo.

Eva picked me up for an evening on the town. We visited several Swiss watch stores, then stopped for dinner around 8 p.m. Eva was Spanish. She had come to Geneva for university studies. During my visit with Steph, she told me it was difficult to live in Switzerland because she thought Swiss culture was racist. I was surprised because I always thought the French people were racist, especially toward Africans. So I was interested in hearing about Switzerland from Eva's perspective.

She talked about how difficult it was for her to live in Switzerland, especially when looking for a decent job. Even as a European living in Switzerland, she felt life was more difficult for those coming from Spain, Portugal, and Turkey. She thought it was also worse for Africans, Latin Americans, and Asians. About midnight, Eva accompanied me back to my hotel and promised to show me other parts of town the next evening.

I slept in the next day and then read some of the books I had received from WHO. I was very interested in the reports of the Alma Ata Conference, where the UN adopted primary health-care strategies for reaching the objective of "Health for

All By 2000." I also read as much as possible on the village health-care strategies developed in China. I wanted to apply some of these strategies in the Kajiji region. The books and magazines I received were good supplements to several textbooks I had shipped to Kinshasa before I left Fresno.

Eva came to pick me up after she got off work so we could eat a last dinner together. We visited until 2 a.m. in the hotel lounge. When we were ready to say goodbye, she asked if she could visit me in Paris after I returned to my brother's place. She was interested in Africa and fascinated by African culture. She had met several African university students but never spent as much time with them as she had with me. I asked her to call me after I returned to Paris. Before she left, she helped me call Steph's sister, Marie Claire, to tell her when I might be arriving in Lyon.

I could feel Eva and I were falling in love, but I had to go. After all, I had not come to Geneva to stay. I had accomplished what I had come for, and it was time to go.

Marie Claire was waiting for me when I arrived in Lyon. She was excited to see me. I felt like I had known her for a long time. She was in her late 20s or early 30s and wore her hair down to her shoulders. In Africa, I would have asked her how old she was, but I remembered this was inappropriate in Europe and North America. She took my backpack and told me she was on vacation and that her sister had asked her to assist me while I was in Lyon.

Once again, I felt like God was sending angels to help me along my way. Marie Claire had made a reservation for me in a small family-owned hotel in the city center. I registered, then she gave me several maps of the city and instructed me on how to use the taxis and buses. I told her my main interest in Lyon was to visit the medical school of the University Claude Bernard. She offered to go there with me the next day.

I didn't realize what it would be like to walk on that campus and to see all the people in their white coats, old and young, women and men. I visited the admissions office, after which we sat on a bench to contemplate the university grounds and people. I felt sad because I had not been able to attend medical school here because of the accident, but I didn't want Marie Claire to know. I asked her if we could leave and find a place for a late lunch, after which I thought I would tell her why I had become so upset. But I didn't have the courage to tell her.

"I think I need to go back to my hotel to rest," I said. "How about meeting at 8 for dinner? Then we can talk more about what happened today."

"No problem," she said. "You know that I am all yours and my schedule is flexible and will depend on yours until we leave for Paris."

She arrived around 7:30 pm. We visited for awhile in the hotel lounge, then took a taxi to her favorite restaurant.

"Can I order one of my favorite wines?" she asked me.

"As long as it is French wine, I will be very happy," I agreed. She ordered a bottle of Bordeaux, which I had learned to like from my brother and his friends in Paris.

We visited for a long time. Finally, she asked me why I had become upset when we visited the university. I said I had been very content with the ways things had turned out in my life professionally. I had gone to the United States with the intention of studying medicine, specializing in surgery, and then going back to work in rural Congo. I told her that my dream was coming true when I decided to study tropical medicine in France.

"You see, I had been accepted to study at the medical school at Claude Bernard University and my accident took place just a few weeks from the time I was getting ready to leave for Lyon," I finally told her. Walking on that campus and seeing all those doctors, nurses, and students in training had raised many old emotions. I told her I felt as if I could have been one of those people on campus, if only things had turned out differently.

"Why didn't you tell anyone there that you had been accepted in their school and explain what had happened to you?" Marie Claire asked me.

"I thought I was courageous, but today I realized that it still pains me to realize that I have followed a different dream than when I first moved to the West," I admitted.

Marie Claire was a good listener. I realized I had not mourned the loss of my dream, although I still was going to work in the health profession. I shed a few tears as we talked and she assured me things were going to be just fine. She encouraged me to continue building professional bridges.

She asked about my experiences in North America. Marie Claire had never traveled to the United States or Canada when I met her. She was hoping to do so, and was curious about the relationship between blacks and whites there. "Did you experience any racism when you studied in the U.S.?" she asked me.

On one hand, I found the question difficult to answer. I also found the answer relatively simple. I never had a problem discussing racial issues while I was in Southern California. Because of the schools and churches I had attended, it was almost impossible to feel discriminated against. I never felt I was a direct target of racism. I lived in a dorm at Fresno, in which four of the eight students in our module were African American, two were African, and two were white.

I told her I had expected to develop excellent relationships with African Americans. Unfortunately, that was never the case. I once asked one of my African American colleagues why we Africans felt more accepted by whites than by African American students on campus. His answer surprised me. He had been taught not to trust Africans because they had been the ones who sold the slaves to the whites centuries before.

I explained to my African American friend that we both had nothing to do with the slave trade, so why should we be suspicious of one another?

The discussion also reminded me of the summer of 1975, when I had worked in North Carolina among African American MB churches. I spent two months living with different black families for a week or two each. While living in Lenoir, North Carolina, I was invited for dinner one evening.

The couple told me I was the first African they had ever hosted. I asked them how they felt about Africans. They told me about the social pain they felt in American culture. Because of their skin color, they still had to go through the back door in certain restaurants and sit at the back of buses and churches. They had their own spaces in parks, while other locations were considered off limits. They also reflected on how Africans were accepted by whites when they visited churches. It made them feel like the Africans were considered superior compared to African Americans. True or not, they also felt like the Africans often expressed their sense of pride in a manner that didn't respect African Americans. I didn't feel they were targeting me individually, but I think I provided them an opportunity to talk about something that had been troubling them for a long time. We laughed together about all the funny ideas we had about each other.

Marie Claire didn't say much as I told her all these stories, but she was still very curious about something. She finally asked me a poignant question. "How about the whites in your churches? Do they accept blacks or people from other racial or ethnic groups? I want you to be honest with me. I am very curious. I read a lot about the racial issues in America and I have watched movies and documentaries on the tensions but never had someone to really discuss them with. Don't hesitate because I am a white woman."

I told her I had spent most of my time in the United States and Canada in predominantly white communities. The churches I attended were almost 100 percent white. When someone from another ethnic background attended, it was usually an international student or a visitor from a partner church in Africa, Asia, or Latin America.

If anything, I felt more shocked about the stereotypes people still harbored toward Africa. Once, when we were watching the famous "Rumble in the Jungle" boxing match between Muhammad Ali and George Foreman, held in Kinshasa in 1974, someone had remarked, "Look, they have cars in Congo."

The closest I came to feeling hurt for racial reasons was when I became a good friend with a church leader's daughter. It was a family for whom I had a lot of respect. Their daughter was one of my classmates and we spent a lot of time together after my accident in 1976. She drove me to different parks around Fresno and we went out to dinner from time to time. I didn't consider our relationship romantic. We just enjoyed spending time together.

One day, she told me her parents didn't think it was good for us to spend time together. I asked her why. She didn't want to say, but when I pushed her, she told me it was because I was African. It was hurtful, not because the family judged me based on my place of origin, but because this was a church leader I had trusted and who had helped train leaders serving in my home country.

Marie Claire was very interested in the racial tension inside North American churches. I didn't feel I could speak to this directly because I had not been exposed to such tension. What I knew was that Sundays were the most segregated days in the whole country. Even in my own denomination, although there were many African Americans and Latinos in the Fresno area, they didn't attend our white churches. Marie Claire was surprised that so many American denominations had been involved in mission work and yet had a hard time including people of other ethnic groups in their churches.

It was almost 1 a.m. when Marie Claire asked me when I wanted to go to Paris. She said she had been planning to go there when Steph asked her to assist me. I had hoped to spend three days in Lyon, but the emotions I had experienced forced me to change my plans. I asked her if we could leave the next day and we agreed to take the night train.

It was so good to travel with someone so knowledgeable about the country. During the trip to Paris, I discovered Marie Claire had been born in Poland and that her family had moved to France when she was a teenager. She was very well traveled, too, especially in Europe. She also wasn't shy about telling me when I did something inappropriate to her culture. Once on our trip, I had ordered sandwiches and two small bottles of red wine. I just opened my sandwich and started eating. Soon after I finished the first half of the sandwich, she asked me why I had eaten the piece with the cheese before the one with beef. I was used to buying sandwiches in the United States where no one thought about such things.

"Is that African or American?" she asked me, and we laughed. Jokingly, I told her that to me, food was just food. I didn't care what I ate first, even if the French thought you must eat the meat before the cheese.

We were about an hour from Paris when she asked me if I had ever smoked a cigar. "Never," I told her.

"Would you like to try?" she asked. She shared about how she smoked a cigar once a year as part of a covenant with a small group of friends. They got together on New Year's Eve, smoked a cigar, and shared a glass of vodka before they left each other's company. I agreed to give it a try when we arrived in Paris. My brother, Tshinabu, was waiting for me when we arrived at the central train station. I introduced Marie Claire to my brother. She and I agreed to meet again before I left Paris for Kinshasa.

My brother suggested we have dinner in his apartment. There were several Congolese living in Paris, and my brother had maintained contact with a few of them. Many were known to be involved in activities he didn't approve of. However, he was always in contact with John Mwanga and his wife, Jeannette, who had studied in the nursing school in Kajiji, and with our cousin, Kaputu. A few minutes after we arrived at Tshinabu's apartment, Jeannette stopped by to check if we needed anything. I was happy to see her because I had known her since high school. I had been in love with her best friend. She offered to make fufu, a common African porridge, for us before she went back home. She promised to come back the next day to help me with anything I needed while Tshinabu was at work. She also invited us to their house for a Congolese meal on Saturday night.

The telephone rang on Thursday night. It was Eva, the young woman I had met in Geneva. She wanted to keep her promise of visiting me before I left for Kinshasa. Tshinabu didn't have any problem with Eva visiting, and she arrived Friday evening. The Latin Quarter where Tshinabu lived had several little cafés, so we went to one of them for dinner. The next day, while Tshinabu was at work, Eva and Jeannette helped me pack for my departure the following week. Jeannette suggested we go directly to her house and said Tshinabu would join us after work.

It was so good to be with Jeannette and her family. We talked about our high school time, living in Kajiji and all the different relationships we had during our teens and why some ended up getting married and others didn't. I asked Jeannette about my former girlfriend, Jolie. She had gotten married, but the relationship had not worked out. She was from a rich family and her dad was in government. My parents discouraged me from continuing a relationship with a girl from a rich family. After all, I was from a pastor's family. Would I have the financial means to take care of her? I also had left to study in the United States and many things were going to change for both of us. Jolie and I loved each other and we never talked about material things.

Jeannette really liked Eva. "She almost gives you the impression of being an African. You should ask her to marry you," Jeannette said in Kituba, so that Eva would not understand her. I said I could not consider marrying someone who had no idea of my culture. We talked about all the good friends I had in North America, but whom I had not considered potential marriage partners. I didn't want an adventurous marriage. I wanted to marry someone, whether African, European, or North American, who was committed to living in rural Africa.

We went back to Tshinabu's place and continued packing my stuff. I could see that Eva was becoming very fond of me. I was fond of her, too, but at the same time, I was afraid of a short-lived romance. She offered to come visit me in Congo after finishing her studies. We exchanged addresses. We spent all day together on Sunday, and then she left in the evening for Geneva.

I met up with Marie Claire for our ceremonial cigar on Wednesday. We talked about meeting again one day if I returned to the region.

On Saturday evening, Tshinabu, Kaputu, and Jeannette accompanied me to the airport, and I left for Kinshasa. I reminisced about my month of travel in Europe, the time I spent with Dr. Morley in London, the woman who helped me tie my shoe in Rome, Steph and Eva and Marie Claire. I thought of Jeannette and her family and my brother, Tshinabu, not knowing when I would see any of them again.

I arrived in Kinshasa early on Sunday morning. I went through all the customs and immigration formalities. I picked up my bags and walked out expecting to find someone waiting to meet me. No one was there.

"Wonderful," I said to myself. "Such a beautiful way of coming back home."

CHAPTER 20

Returning to My Homeland

1980

I had been invited to speak in a couple of churches in the Seattle, Washington, area and Linda took some time off work so we could travel together. We had decided to visit some former missionaries to Congo who were then living in British Columbia. One person I was interested in spending time with was Katie Penner. I had known her since my childhood.

I had a lot of respect for Katie. She worked for many years in Kajiji, and then was invited to lead the nursing department at the general hospital in Kinshasa, a state-run medical center named after President Mobutu's mother.

Several years after she had returned to Canada, she was asked to go back to Kajiji to assist with a new nurses' training program. Katie could work with government and church institutions without any apparent conflict. She had respect for government and church leaders. She also impressed me because although she knew me and other local leaders as children and gave us our childhood vaccines, she still could work under our guidance in Kajiji. I had not seen her for many years when we visited her in a Kelowna, British Columbia, nursing home.

"She has been waiting for you since yesterday," a social worker said. Katie looked beautiful as she smiled when we walked in. I noticed this was the first time I had seen her wearing jewelry, but I didn't comment on it because it didn't matter. It was just good to see her looking so well.

We visited for a couple of hours in her room. She asked how things were in Congo and especially in Kajiji. Although she repeated herself many times, Katie was still sharp. We updated her on the situation at the nursing school and about some of the nurses she would have known. We also talked about former missionaries. After we ate lunch with her at the nursing home, Linda wheeled her back to her room and I stayed to visit with one of the workers.

"She is a special person. We really like having Katie here," the woman told me. "I have read the book she wrote on her experience in Congo and I am now asking all my colleagues and friends to read it."

"I know, she is a wonderful person," I said. "You can be assured that Katie will continue to have a positive influence on people until her days on Earth are over."

Linda had already left for the car when I walked back to Katie's room. She asked me to sit next to her.

"I felt very alone after Elsie died," she said, referring to another woman who had been a nurse in Congo and a lifelong friend. "Now I feel trapped in this place. I don't have any independence."

I also had worked with Elsie, who died from breast cancer after she returned to Oregon from Africa. She had been my supervisor when I worked on my thesis for my master's in public health.

For a moment as I held her hand, I thought of all that Katie had done when I was a child, teaching Sunday school classes, establishing the nurses' training program, and reorganizing the nursing department of the Kinshasa hospital. She was my mentor when we worked together in the 1980s, and yet when I went to visit her after work, she became like another mother to me, just as she had been when I was a child.

Here in Kelowna, although surrounded by many caring people, she was feeling trapped. I felt tears in my eyes as I looked at her. I felt the pain she was going through. I had lived that same life of pain several years earlier because of my car accident. I loved Katie and I could not bear the pain of watching her in that situation.

"I need to go," I told her. "I think Linda is waiting for me in the car because we have dinner with Murray and Faith Nickel in Abbotsford today, and we have about four hours yet to drive." I could tell she didn't want me to leave. She kissed me goodbye, then asked me to write her, even short notes.

"I feel alone here and I would appreciate hearing from you," she added as she watched me leave her room and disappear down the long hallway. I had been happy to see her, but I was now feeling sick to my stomach. I didn't want to leave her, but I had to go, not sure if I would ever see her again.

As we drove back to Abbotsford, I continued to think about Katie and the public health work in Congo. We worked at improving the nutritional status of women and children. We provided vaccinations for pregnant women and children under 5. We introduced new and improved nutrition, including manioc and peanuts. We felt good about our accomplishments. Several young North Americans worked with us under our nutrition, public health, and nurses' training programs. We even received a couple of young medical students during their last year of medical training in the United States and Canada.

Dr. Roger Fast, one of my former colleagues in this work, joined me for my January 2007 trip to Congo. We spent many hours talking about how awful the situation was in Kajiji. The quality of care had dropped, medicine was limited in the pharmacy, and the hospital was empty. In a way, several years later and with both of us now living in Fresno, we were discouraged but still hoped to make a difference.

Working in public health in Congo in the 1980s was exciting and energizing. The program of broad social reforms that President Mobutu had declared during the 1970s had failed. Mobutu had promised Congo would rank first economically in Africa. The Congolese people lived with high hopes for a better future. Even in rural areas, people talked about how the government would build roads and schools across the country, hospitals would be fully stocked with medicine, and every Congolese would be able to purchase a car.

After all, the Cold War was playing to Mobutu's advantage. The prices on the world market for copper and gold were high. Mobutu was a hero wherever he went. When I left Congo in December 1973, the Congolese currency was equal to $2 U.S. Politically, Mobutu was in control. He established MPR—the Popular Revolutionary Movement—as the country's only political party. Every Congolese citizen was automatically a member of the party. According to Mobutu, even unborn and newborn babies were considered members of MPR. They didn't have a choice.

Mobutu didn't feel threatened by any so-called opposition, inside or outside the country. Almost none of his political enemies had a strong financial basis, so Mobutu could buy them off at any time.

Mobutu also developed an excellent security system. Many undercover agents were hired to monitor situations that could destabilize his political standing. A level of fear reigned among the population because one never knew who would report you if you said anything that might be perceived as opposing the government, especially remarks against Mobutu or his family. Many people were arrested and tortured, even in rural areas, simply because they had insulted the president. You also could be arrested for moving while the Congolese flag was being raised or lowered, considered a major offense against the state. The arresting officers also could make things worse by accusing you of resisting arrest or insulting the president in the process.

Despite all this, Mobutu was fostering a sense of pride in Congo. After a trip to China, Mobutu nationalized all the country's institutions and enterprises. European merchants were asked to turn over their enterprises or face deportation within 48 hours. Citizens were required to adopt exclusively African names. Mobutu didn't want to hear any so-called Christian names. Private schools, especially parochial ones, which were more than half the schools in the country, were nationalized, with all principals nominated by the government. Mobutu called for equality for all religions and would not conceive of the Roman Catholic Church being politically privileged in comparison to Protestant faiths because of historical ties with the Belgian government. Ironically, the mood in the country was one of joy and freedom, even in a police state, because the Congolese people finally felt free from colonial powers and influences.

The honeymoon, however, didn't last long. By the end of the 1970s, the economy was starting to deteriorate. School and health systems were falling apart. The inflation rate was more than 100 percent. The government wasn't meeting its payroll and most people who depended on government salaries started to go hungry. School and medical fees became difficult for most people to pay. Katanga, a region in southern Congo rich in minerals that provided more than half the government's budget, tried to secede. It was amid all this that I returned home in 1980 to work in public health.

CHAPTER 21

Reconnecting in Kajiji

1980s

Soon after I returned to Kinshasa, I started reconnecting with old friends and MB church leaders. I lived for several days with Pastor Masolo Mununga, the regional legal representative in Kinshasa. He helped me connect with many institutions, including Mission Aviation Fellowship, the Church of Christ of Zaire (ECZ), and the Medical Commission of the Church of Christ of Zaire.

One morning, Pastor Masolo took me to the MAF office to visit with Pastor Mukanza, a Mennonite minister working with MAF. He wanted to bring together the three Mennonite church conferences in the country to seek unity on theology and doctrine, peacebuilding, and conflict management.

While at MAF, I met John Kliewer. John was born in the former Belgian Congo and his parents were longtime MB missionaries. I also knew John while I was in high school, when he was my teacher before returning to the United States for further studies. After finishing his pilot's training, he returned to Congo to work for MAF. Our fathers also had worked together.

I admired John a great deal. During my high school years, he picked up students from different mission stations and drove them to the church high school in Kikwit. One Christmas, he took a group of his teacher friends to Kajiji in a small pickup and offered to take me along so I could be with my family. He probably never imagined what that gesture meant to my family and me.

That day in the office, John once again did something that assisted me in getting better acquainted with the future of the health-care system in Congo. He told me about Dr. Dan Fountain, an American Baptist missionary working at the Vanga hospital in Bandundu province. I had heard about Dan when I visited the Medical Commission of the World Council of Churches in Geneva, Switzerland. John suggested I visit Dan before going to Kajiji. "I have one small problem," I said. "I don't have any money to pay for the flight to Vanga."

I had gone back to Congo without any financial backing from anyone. I trusted I would be able to develop grant proposals for my support. I wasn't a missionary, so the MB mission agency could not support me financially.

John said he would take me to Vanga next time he flew there, and promised to make all the arrangements with the Fountain family.

The Baptists had built Vanga, a beautiful mission station, along the Kwilu River. As with most mission stations, it included primary and secondary schools, a hospital, and community development projects. Everything was built around the church, with communities in the region depending on the medical and educational services provided by the church. There were many houses built for the missionaries, teachers, hospital staff, and community development workers. With a grant from a German organization, the church built several extensions for the hospital. The hospital's work included surgical training for new graduates of Congolese medical schools.

Dan and Miriam Fountain's house was located near the river. The house was so close to the river that the whole family went down to the water to bathe each day. I was the only one who took showers in the house, due to my physical limitations.

Dan taught me a key lesson in public health not covered during my formal training—advocacy on the local, regional, and national levels. The second day I was with the Fountains, Dan told me he had been invited to Bulungu, capital of the Kwilu region, to meet with President Mobutu about health care. Mobutu was very clever. Whenever he traveled, in order to boost his image among the Congolese people, he gave "gifts" to local institutions.

In this case, Dan was supposed to tell the president about the work of the hospital and then, out of official goodwill, Mobutu could decide to give a gift of money or materials to the facility. It was great to watch Dan, this man of God, respectfully interact with government leaders. Dan wasn't naïve when he went to see the president, and he realized his position gave him access to many high-level leaders. He knew how to open doors that might otherwise remain closed.

In this region, Dan and his colleagues were trying to decentralize health-care delivery away from the hospital and more toward the local health centers, where more than 80 percent of the health problems could be addressed.

They were developing village health committees responsible for promoting water sanitation, organizing vaccination campaigns, and, in some cases, Bible studies. It reminded me of similar approaches I had seen taken in rural China.

After I had spent a week with Dan, John picked me up in the MAF plane and flew me back to Kajiji.

I was concerned it might be difficult to gain professional acceptance in the town where I was born and grew up. As Jesus had said, no one is ever recognized as a prophet in his own hometown. I sometimes thought of this expression as a good reason not to share my professional skills in Kajiji.

But I learned that working in one's home region could have many benefits. In Kajiji, I was among people I knew and who would be more tolerant of any mistakes I might make. In addition, having my family nearby provided emotional support not available elsewhere.

When I returned to work in Kajiji following my studies abroad, I arrived on a beautiful August afternoon, to be welcomed by a crowd of several hundred men, women, and children, including my parents and many childhood friends. When they had last seen me, four years earlier, I was still in a wheelchair. It was an emotional time for my family and the whole community. Many tears were shed. Now I was walking with a cane, and I had come back not for a visit but to live and work among them. Women and children from the community sang and waved flowers and palm branches as we walked to my parents' house.

It was good to be home again. I was ready to taste my mother's cooking, which I had missed while I had been away. My cousin, Mahungu, said a dinner had been planned for that evening, where people from the community joined my family in welcoming me back.

Soon after my arrival, I was introduced to Dr. Fokum and his family. He originally was from Cameroon but had received his medical training in Kinshasa. He was also the first non-North American doctor to work full time at the Kajiji hospital.

My dad thanked everyone for joining the family on this special occasion of welcoming back not just a Tshimika's son, but a son of the community willing to work among his own people.

The welcome was in my parents' home. The meal was simple, but it was special. It included, beef, pork, chicken, and *sakasaka* (greens similar to spinach and made from manioc leaves). Dessert included bananas, roasted peanuts, a cake made by one of the missionary's cooks, and coffee and tea. As soon as I tasted all this, I knew I was really home.

At the end of the evening, I learned I would be staying with the Fokum family because the hospital didn't have a house for me yet. They were going to discuss my housing situation later. Maybe I wasn't such a hometown prophet after all. I couldn't understand how they didn't have housing for me when they had known for a long time that I had agreed to come back and work in Kajiji.

Though angry about this at first, I quickly got over it. I figured Dr. Fokum might be dealing with his own issues of being an outsider in Kajiji. Now here I was, the first Congolese to work in a leadership role in the hospital.

The time I lived with the Fokum family turned out to be wonderful. They had two children, a girl and a boy to whom my parents became surrogate grandparents. I found out later that life had not been easy for the Fokums in Kajiji. First, his wife wasn't African, but Haitian. Being in Kajiji required an adjustment for both of them, but even more for her. My mother provided her a safe place to go for counsel or just to talk.

Dr. Fokum, like many young doctors finishing their university studies in Congo, didn't have much experience in surgery. In addition, he didn't have much technical support, such as in a university clinic or a hospital with other physicians to rely upon. He was fortunate to have one nurse who had been trained in routine surgery and emergency cesarean sections. However, it wasn't an ideal situation when a newly graduated physician had to learn clinical skills from a nurse.

Dr. Fokum asked me to accompany him a couple times when he was called at night to perform C-sections. He was a very dedicated physician who prayed with each patient before he operated. Because a few women had died during surgery, people in the region became wary any time a woman was brought in for a C-section. Once, when they brought in a certain young woman to have her child delivered, almost all the women in the community stayed home from work. More than 30 women sat outside the operating section of the hospital, waiting for news of the surgery.

As soon as the baby was delivered, one of the nurses announced to the women that it was a girl. A shout rose from the crowd, followed by singing. There was even more joy when they found out that the mother was fine.

Dr. Fokum remained in Kajiji until my cousin Matshifi finished his physician's training and was hired to work there. They worked together for awhile before Dr. Fokum left for Kinshasa and eventually Cameroon, where he worked for one of the biggest mission hospitals in the country. Later Matshifi would be joined by Dr. Roger Fast.

The 1980s were also a good time to be in Kajiji because it was a period when many of our community's young people, who had gone away to college, decided to come back home. I was impressed by how many university graduates were living in this small community of less than 1,000 people. My childhood friend, Funda, was a principal at one of the two

Dr. Roger Fast and a mobile medical clinic in Congo.

high schools in Kajiji, and Matshifi was a physician at the hospital. There also were several Mennonite Central Committee volunteers working in the high school and in community development projects. Being part of a group of young people working for a common cause was energizing.

After a couple months of living with the Fokums, I requested my own place. I wanted a place where I could have my own guests and where my schedule didn't depend on someone else. I joined a Bible study group that Dr. Fokum started with nurses and teachers.

Finally, I got my own place. It was small, but big enough for myself and my sister, Tshamba; my cousin, Lucienne; and Annie, the niece my future wife Linda and I later adopted as our own daughter. It was one of three small houses built for nurses. It had three rooms, and I invested some of my own money to fix it up. We added a kitchen, turned one room into an indoor bathroom, fixed another as an office, and added a room for Tshamba, Annie, and Lucienne.

Fridays in our house were fun. With the Bible study group we also began to play the card game UNO each weekend. I taught the group how to play dominoes, and we started a lengthy tournament with the winner having to wash dishes and the losers buying meat for the victory celebration.

Eventually, I won the tournament and the celebration was held in my house. One thing the others didn't realize was that my sister Tshamba and my cousin Lucienne washed the dishes the next day. I ended up not doing anything except enjoying the fact that I had beaten everyone.

CHAPTER 22

Advocacy Work

1980s

In the early 1980s, Congo joined other UN member nations to make primary health care a main reform strategy for its population. Universal health care was the objective agreed upon by the UN at a 1976 meeting in Alma Ata, now known as Almaty, in present-day Kazakhstan. The idea was to make primary health care economically, socially, culturally, and politically accessible to the majority of the population by the year 2000.

When I arrived in Kinshasa at the end of July 1980, the national ministry of health was just developing its primary health-care strategies. In 1982, the ministry of health published *"Action Sanitaire* 1982-1986," a document that described the development of a decentralized health-care delivery system. The notion of "health zones" was adopted as the strategic way of decentralizing health-care delivery in Congo.

Each health zone served a population of about 125,000 people. Health zones included a hospital for referral services, a health zone office for technical coordination and supervision, and typically 10 to 20 health areas, depending on population density. Each health area included a health center to provide preventive and curative services and was run by a public health nurse. Outreach activities from the health center in collaboration with the community provided immunizations and growth monitoring for every child.

Subdividing the country into health zones wasn't as easy as one would have imagined. The idea was to use physical features such as rivers and main roads to draw the boundaries. It was also understood that the division took into consideration various cultural issues, because the services provided had to be not only economically but politically and socially accessible. The divisions became a political threat to some politicians. Under this system, each person counted, especially during election time. Moving a boundary line only a short distance could mean several thousand people being moved to another political district.

I recall a long debate in Bandundu province, where I was invited to participate in dividing the region into several health zones. I thought we were dealing with health issues, but then realized I had to take positions that protected certain interests of the population in the region where I grew up. Political issues were so ingrained in the minds of those participating that I soon realized how naïve I had been. But my arguments were strong enough that the provincial and national health authorities agreed to draw the lines as I had proposed.

Two years later, I became supervisor of public work for the Kajiji health zone. Kamwimba, our administrative secretary, was traveling with me as we looked at village health workers' activities and visited the 10 health centers we had organized in the region. I was meeting with a group of local leaders when I got a message that Kamwimba had been arrested by order of the head of the government post.

"He is being accused of sitting down and not wearing a shirt when they were raising the flag," I was told. We drove to the government post and were told the chief already had gone home and was done with all official visits for the day. I decided to drive to his house.

The chief was sitting in a gazebo where he visited with people when he didn't want to go to the office. He came out to welcome us and ordered his workers to bring us two bottles of Coca-Cola. It was warm, but good enough to quench our thirst.

I told him my concern about Kamwimba's arrest. He listened carefully. "You know that your administrative secretary has no respect for the symbol of this country," he told me. I replied that Kamwimba was an honest man and I could not imagine him doing anything disrespectful to the nation.

"Are you telling me that I am a liar?" he asked me.

"I didn't imply that at all, Your Honor," I answered him. It was important for me to address him politely. Many of these political leaders had a strong desire to feel important. Many of them were not qualified for the jobs they held, but had landed them anyway because of who they knew. I said if he would let us do our work well, he would get the credit because it was his administrative region.

He smiled and laughed as I continued to give my little speech about how it was important for politicians to facilitate the job of the medical professional. After he listened to me, he sent someone to ask the police to free Kamwimba. As we talked, I found out his arrest had nothing to do with not standing while they raised the flag. It had to do with my position during the drawing of the local health zones. I had pushed for several villages to be annexed to Kajiji and some of them were from this chief's region. The second reason was that our team had traveled by helicopter and landed in many villages, but didn't land in his parents' village. "I couldn't punish you, so I got your administrative secretary," he finally admitted.

When I returned to Congo following my education, I had hoped to help plan public programs that included health and nutrition education, family planning, and management of primary health care. Before long, I realized I spent most of my time advocating either for institutions I worked for, the local population, or individuals being threatened by local government leaders.

My work almost landed me in jail, and at the highest level of my country's cruel security system. Most people perceived me as patient and tolerant. However, I soon discovered how intolerant I could be, especially toward anyone I felt was taking advantage of others considered weak.

Almost all the government leaders in the Kajiji area, with the exception of those in the military, were usually from the local region. The military leaders were sometimes the most notorious for abusing the population, especially medical patients from Angola. The hospital provided service to 150,000 people without counting patients who came from Angola or other parts of the country. Angola was at war, so many people from border villages in Angola came to Kajiji for health care. Another reason for coming to Kajiji was that many of the Angolans had relatives in the region. Almost all the villages on both sides of the border between Congo and Angola were once part of the Lunda Kingdom. In some ways, these people were still seeking assistance within their traditional geographic area. They were now Congolese and Angolans because the white men had decided they were. So why would the local government leaders on the Congolese side, knowing that these were their kin, harass them like they were total strangers?

Once I was returning from lunch when one of the nurses walked into my office with a worried look. "We have several policemen in the surgical ward who want to take one of the patients that the doctor operated on yesterday," she said.

"Do you know who sent them?" I asked.

"They said the local political chief sent them, and they need to take the man to the government office," she said.

I could feel my body becoming very tense. I wanted to leave for the surgical ward, but I decided not to because I caught myself thinking about hitting one of them with my cane.

"Can you please ask them to come to my office?" I asked the nurse.

I leaned over my desk as I thought about how to talk with these policemen without making a fool of myself. Five of them walked in with the nurse. They explained that the political chief had asked them to bring this man in because he was a foreigner and needed to register before he could be admitted to the hospital. I asked them if they knew the man had been operated on the day before. I also asked them how they would feel if I forced one of their close relatives to walk three miles only 24 hours after a surgery during which the doctor had amputated his leg.

"I am asking you to leave the hospital premises," I finally told them angrily. "Go tell whoever sent you that I kicked you out. If he wants to, he can send you together with some soldiers to arrest me."

I didn't want to give them a chance to say more. They walked out of my office, and I asked the nurse to notify me if these policemen showed up again. I lived next to the hospital, so it wasn't going to be hard for them to find me.

There were a couple of issues at play here. I had received instructions from immigration officials asking us to keep track of all the patients from Angola. Each time we sent them our monthly reports, we also sent copies to all the local government offices. The local chief knew it, but in this case he had heard that this man had a large diamond that he had brought from Angola to sell in Congo. He wanted to get part of the money.

I didn't hear from the chief about this for a long time. I did, however, see him a couple of times during some official events, which many of us were required to attend. He didn't seem to be angry for how I had treated his men. A couple of months later, I found out he had written a long letter to the government security offices accusing me as a national security threat. He recommended that I be arrested and sent to the most notorious prison in the country. He sent copies to many provincial and national offices, but not to me, the accused.

I asked the gentleman who brought me the letter what I should do. He suggested I write the chief a letter with copies to all those offices, because he felt the provincial and national authorities were more inclined to believe me. He also insisted I send a copy to the presidential security office.

"I don't deal with those folks," I said. "And how could I even send the letter when we don't have post offices that work?" My friend offered to assist me in sending all the letters if I wrote to the chief.

I first wrote a seven-page letter full of anger. I gave it to my wife, Linda, and a couple of other trusted friends to read.

"I don't think you should send this letter the way you have written it," Linda said. "You will become like him if you send it the way it is. You have to show him that you are wiser than him. I would suggest that you set it aside a few days. Then we can work at it together when you are not angry and your secretary can type it afterward." That's exactly what we did.

I gave the revised letter to my friend so he could assist me in delivering the copies. The chief didn't answer me, so I waited to see if I heard from anyone else.

Three months later, I received a small handwritten note in French. It said: "Little brother Pakisa, I will be making a tour of the whole province before too long. I would like to take time visiting you and your work in the Kajiji area." The note was signed "your big brother, Nsambia," governor of the Bandundu province. I had met him once during an official military maneuver in the Kahemba region where all the top military officers and provincial authorities had come for a closing ceremony.

I had taken my father and two other Kajiji pastors to the ceremony, which was held about 60 miles from Kajiji. That evening, I was invited to a private reception for the military officers and the governor. President Mobutu was supposed to attend, but he decided not to come. Many were disappointed because he had never visited that region during his time in power. I told the organizers I would only go if my dad and his two colleagues also could attend. That evening, I met the governor and most of Mobutu's top generals.

When the governor finally came to visit our area, he refused to stay in the house the local government people had arranged for him. He asked me to organize housing for him and his staff, which I did. I invited him for coffee while we waited for the official banquet organized by the local government leaders. That evening he informed me about the letter he had received from the chief and said he had read my response. He said he had discussed both letters with President Mobutu, who asked him to talk to me in person.

"You are not a threat to our national security," he assured me. He went on to say that he received strict orders from Mobutu to make sure the chief didn't harass me anymore. He told me the work of the Kajiji hospital often had been an object of discussion between Mobutu and Jose Eduardo dos Santos, his counterpart in Angola, especially around the border issue. Mobutu always reminded his colleague about how many Angolans are taken care of at the Kajiji hospital.

Two days later, the governor called his staff together for a security briefing while they were traveling. He invited me to attend and gave strict orders to the security agents, the local police, and the chief to make sure I was left alone to do my work. He went as far as to inform them that if I wasn't working for the church, the president had suggested I be transferred to Equateur, to work in Mobutu's home province.

The chief never harassed me again. Last time I saw him was in Kinshasa. He was very sick with tuberculosis and didn't have money for medical treatment. I went to see him and gave him some money so he could see a doctor and buy medicine he needed. The governor, on the last day before he left, took me aside. He asked me to talk with my dad and find out if my family had a difficult history with the chief that would explain why he had been after me. This led to my learning two important lessons.

First, I learned we were related on my mother's side. His mother had been a slave that my family had inherited but freed. This meant that culturally, her children were not to be considered slaves anymore. Why was he being mean to me then?

Second, I was puzzled by the way some of our church leaders understood what it meant to be a peace church. While working on this conflict, I asked several church leaders to advise me. One of the pastors suggested we should not challenge those in power because, as members of an Anabaptist church, we were called to be nonviolent and to live at peace with government leaders. I answered that I didn't agree. I said I wouldn't obey any government leaders who endangered the lives of people created in God's image, especially for personal gain.

I asked my father if he agreed with what the other pastor had said. He didn't, and assured me I was doing the right thing. He counseled me to consider whether my actions were motivated by personal fear or were the right thing to do given the circumstances. My father was a fearless man, so I wasn't surprised by his advice.

CHAPTER 23

My Mennonite Connections

2000–2009

"Are you really a Mennonite?" The man who asked this question was sitting next to me at Dulles International Airport near Washington, D.C., as we waited for our flight to San Francisco. I was returning to Fresno from Akron, Pennsylvania, where I had been attending Mennonite Central Committee annual meetings.

I am always amazed by how people respond when I tell them I'm a Mennonite. In some ways, I shouldn't be surprised because there are many Mennonites who recently have emigrated from Europe who cannot believe there are such creatures in the world as African Mennonites.

"Why do you ask? What does a Mennonite look like to you?" I responded.

"The Mennonites I know do not dress like you," the man said. "They are whites and many of them drive buggies and live in Pennsylvania and Ohio, and some in Kansas and Oklahoma."

"You're right, but that is only one piece of the puzzle," I said. "You're thinking only of the white Mennonites. We are a quilt made of many brothers, sisters, and cousins from around the world.

"There are more than a million Mennonites worldwide and the majority of them are in Africa, Asia, and Latin America. As a matter of fact, I am from the Democratic Republic of

Congo, where you'll find more than 25 percent of Mennonites worldwide."

Next, my new friend wanted to know what Mennonites believed, given our diversity. He also asked me how a Congolese could even become Mennonite.

Once, I would have had a difficult time explaining what Mennonites hold in common. I have tried to explain it in light of our peace stance, or by describing how we are a Christ-centered church that embraces discipleship and mutual aid. Some with whom I shared that explanation were not always convinced this was so particular to Mennonites. Many other churches and even many non-church groups share some of our convictions on nonviolence, after all.

Thanks to my work with Mennonite World Conference (MWC), I was able to give my friend a document published by MWC in 2006. I explained that as far I knew, this was the first time Mennonite and Brethren in Christ churches from around the world had agreed on what they believe and what holds us together as a family of faith. I offered him these seven "Shared Convictions."

1. God is known to us as Father, Son, and Holy Spirit, the Creator who seeks to restore fallen humanity by calling a people to be faithful in fellowship, worship, service, and witness.

2. Jesus is the Son of God. Through his life and teachings, his cross and resurrection, he showed us how to be faithful disciples, redeemed the world, and offers eternal life.

3. As a church, we are a community of those whom God's Spirit calls to turn from sin, acknowledge Jesus Christ as Lord, receive baptism upon confession of faith, and follow Christ in life.

4. As a faith community, we accept the Bible as our authority for faith and life, interpreting it together under Holy Spirit guidance, in the light of Jesus Christ, to discern God's will for our obedience.

5. The Spirit of Jesus empowers us to trust God in all areas of life so we become peacemakers who renounce violence, love our enemies, seek justice, and share our possessions with those in need.

6. We gather regularly to worship, to celebrate the Lord's Supper, and to hear the Word of God in a spirit of mutual accountability.

7 As a world-wide community of faith and life, we transcend boundaries of nationality, race, class, gender, and language. We seek to live in the world without conforming to the powers of evil, witnessing to God's grace by serving others, caring for creation, and inviting all people to know Jesus Christ as Savior and Lord.

In these convictions we draw inspiration from Anabaptist forebears of the 16th century, who modeled radical discipleship to Jesus Christ. We seek to walk in his name by the power of the Holy Spirit, as we confidently await Christ's return and the final fulfillment of God's kingdom.

My friend started to laugh as I was explaining to him about the long process MWC went through to develop this crucial document. "So it took you guys that many years to develop and agree on something that explains who you are, when you are known to be so strong on peace and reconciliation?" my friend chuckled.

"I guess, after all, we are just as human as you are despite our piety," I observed.

I also explained how I had become a Mennonite in Congo. I told him the country was carved and distributed among different Protestant groups in the same way the whole of Africa was divided by Europeans in the early 19th century. The colonial power decided that in order to avoid conflict among different Protestant churches, each group evangelized only in a given area of the country. That also meant each group evangelized a specific tribal group. In some ways, that evangelism strategy forced Congolese people to undergo several phases of conversion.

The first phase was for the Congolese who came in contact with the missionaries to accept Christ and deny their old ways of life. They didn't have a choice about becoming Mennonite, Baptist, Presbyterian, Covenant, or part of an Unevangelized Tribal Mission church. That decision was made by the colonial power. Another option was to become Catholic because the Roman Catholic Church was allowed to establish its congregations anywhere, as long as their mission stations were not located near Protestant outposts.

In the case of my family, it was the Unevangelized Tribal Mission that brought the gospel to our area. When this mission declared bankruptcy in the United States, its work was taken over by the Mennonite Brethren.

The second phase of conversion involved personal choices about theological and doctrinal engagement. Up to then, the Congolese had accepted the theology and doctrine of the Protestant church assigned to a particular region. With personal study and research, and as people began to travel more widely, many Congolese started making their own decisions about which denomination they joined, instead of abiding by the will of the colonial powers.

My friend listened very carefully, then asked if the colonial powers really had that much control over people in Congo. I could see he didn't know much about African history, but I was happy that one more person was interested in our church's story. I told him my father was an MB pastor in Congo. He worked until he was 85 years old and helped establish many churches in southern Bandundu province.

My father died early one morning after a very busy Sunday. He had participated in a blessing ceremony of 12 children in his congregation in Kajiji. Was that number symbolic or what? That same morning, he participated in a monthly communion service, then held a meeting of congregational leaders. That night, he started to experience severe pain in his right shoulder. He was taken to the hospital around 11:30 p.m., and at midnight, he had a massive heart attack and died after saying, "Jesus, Jesus, Jesus!"

"I am sorry," my friend said.

"Oh no, don't be sorry," I replied. "My dad lived a good life, so I don't regret anything. I am just afraid that in many ways I am becoming more and more like him."

"Did you say that you had worked for several Mennonite agencies?" my friend continued. "I am curious if they really accept you as a colleague with something to offer to the work and ministries, or were you just a puppet for all these white people?"

I didn't get the chance to answer because someone came to escort me to the aircraft.

CHAPTER 24

MBMS International and Memisa

1992–2001

I was at a conference on missions in Elkhart, Indiana, in the late 1980s when I met Dave Dyck, the new director of programs for MB Mission and Service (MBMS) International. He asked me what I was planning on doing after my studies at Loma Linda University ended in 1991. I told him my intention was to go back to Africa, but that I had student loans I needed to pay back. He didn't offer me a job, but we visited several times again during the conference. Right away I liked Dave.

I liked him even more when I found out he was a brother to Ernie Dyck, a longtime missionary in Congo when it was still known as Zaire. I had many fond memories of Ernie from when I was living away from home in Kikwit during my high school days. Just like I had done in Kajiji, I also wanted to find a way to make a living so my parents didn't have to send me money. So I asked Ernie during my senior year if he could find me a job in Kikwit.

Ernie recommended me as a language tutor to several of the North American volunteers teaching in my school or involved in community development programs. I spent several hours a week tutoring them in the Kituba dialect and got paid every two weeks. Ernie also gave me a weekly allowance of five liters of kerosene that I used in a lamp that Sarah Peters and Arlen Gerdes, two other missionaries in Kajiji, helped me purchase so I could study at night.

"Would you like to accompany us to Congo in a couple months?" Dave asked. He wanted me to interpret not only what was being said, but also the deeper meaning behind the words. The trip was very revealing of how church leaders and mission representatives worked together. I was amazed by how deeply hidden agendas influenced these meetings. Take, for instance, a request by the Congo MB Conference to have North American churches send three missionary advisers to work in the Kinshasa, Kikwit, and Kajiji/Panzi regions.

"Why do you want North American advisers when you are mature enough to conduct all the church business without missionaries?" the general secretary for MBMS International asked. The church leaders decided to reflect on the question. They murmured among themselves while asking me not to translate their discussion. According to these leaders, the only way they could expect financial assistance from the North American churches was if these churches had one of their own in the country. They also talked about how having these advisers guaranteed their transportation. The missionaries had vehicles; the locals didn't.

As requested, I didn't translate this part of the discussion. I laughed as I listened, but I saw that Dave was curious. I whispered that I would tell him what was being said when we were alone in the guesthouse later.

"Why didn't they just ask for vehicles or drivers?" the general secretary asked.

"I think they were just playing your game the best way they knew how," I said. Soon after we returned to North America, MBMS International purchased a vehicle for the Congolese church's central office.

When I finished my doctoral studies at Loma Linda University, MBMS International asked me to return to Congo to coordinate the church's health and development program. Dave was ready to work with me on a financial package that made it possible for me to repay my loans as well as save some for travel to the United States every three years to visit Linda's family. On January 1, 1992, I left for Kinshasa, but Linda stayed behind temporarily because of a spate of violence in the big cities.

During the 1990s, the economic situation in Congo was deteriorating and many workers who depended on the government for support were not being paid. I was asked to live in Kikwit rather than Kajiji. Water and electricity were not reliable and the roads were bad. You needed a four-wheel drive vehicle to travel in many parts of the city.

We were asked to organize the coordination office for health and development activities under the *Departement de Sante et de Development Communautaire*, or DESADEC (French for the Department of Health and Community Development), and integrate it with the central office of the MB conference in Kikwit. I hired two young members of the MB church to work with me.

The role of DESADEC was to oversee a dozen health centers in the Kikwit region; a professional school in Kinshasa that trained young people in carpentry and masonry work; the Kajiji health zone with one hospital, 17 health centers and one nursing school; and a couple of houses in the Kikwit and Kajiji areas.

The church's office in Kikwit seemed like an abandoned, haunted house. I was told that most leaders came to the office only when they received financial subsidies from the churches in North America. We hired a couple of young men to clean the building and reopened the water system. I met a couple of Americans who were running a sawmill and doing road repair, and asked them to help remove old car and truck bodies that had been left in the yard.

This made the church office visible not only in the city but to visitors from elsewhere. Church members had high expectations when we organized DESADEC, but the extreme poverty made our work difficult.

Many people expected the church to solve their social and economic problems. After all, the churches had organized schools, hospitals, and other community development programs. So when things fell apart nationally, people expected the church to step in.

The office in Kikwit became very busy with visitors from other churches and NGOs working in Bandundu province. For three years, DESADEC was elected to preside over the board of the provincial consortium of non-governmental organizations (NGOs) and established partnerships with Oxfam, the Kikwit Catholic Diocese, and other groups.

In the meantime, MBMS International decided to regionalize its administration. During one of his visits to Congo in 1993, Dave Dyck informed the local MB leadership that his agency was looking for an African to serve as regional secretary for the Africa program. Several months later, I was offered the job and became the first non-North American to hold that position. Due to logistical and communication problems and the need to be in regular contact with the Fresno and Winnipeg offices, I moved my family to Kinshasa in 1994. I had two countries to oversee, Congo and Angola.

Working for MBMS International from 1994 to 2001 was fascinating. I enjoyed my role as an ambassador for the church. When meeting with the church leadership in Africa, I defended North American policies, and when in North America, I defended the cause of the Congolese and Angolan churches. Whenever Dave Dyck or general director Harold Ens visited Congo, they always emphasized that I was the program director for the Africa programs and that their presence didn't minimize my role. That was new to many people in our churches. They were used to the local leader being pushed aside whenever the higher boss arrived.

The churches in Congo and Angola were used to working with white people and some of the leaders had a difficult time believing one of their own could actually defend their

The author speaking at a general assembly of the Congo Mennonite Brethren Church in Kikwit, Congo, in the mid-1990s.

cause in America. Unfortunately, although I was Congolese, some still perceived me as one of the white people because I had lived and studied abroad. Many in Kikwit also thought I was American. Some thought I worked for the Central Intelligence Agency because I had several antennas on the top of my house—one for our short-wave radio set and another for our two-way radio. After a long discussion, my friend Pascal convinced my neighbor that I was from Congo and could speak the local language. With time, this businessman and his family became some of my best friends in Kikwit.

Church leaders also were used to receiving financial subsidies from MBMS International, so if they asked me to send a message requesting funds and I told them the budgeting process was closed, some of them perceived it as an African blocking them from receiving money from the white men.

One day while I was attending a church leadership meeting in Kikwit, I was approached by a delegation from the Roman Catholic medical NGO, Memisa Medicus Mundi.

"My name is Frere Luc," said their leader, a Capuchin priest. "I live in Kinshasa, but I am accompanying a Memisa delegation from Belgium. They are here to explore the possibility of supporting several Bandundu province health zones. We were wondering if you could join us for a short meeting at the Kikwit Diocese's office."

The meeting went well. I could tell the team had only a general idea of the health-care system in Congo. As an institution supported by Catholics, I was impressed that they were willing to consider assisting health zones co-sponsored by Protestant churches. We discussed the different health projects they could support, and they asked me to join them in Kinshasa for further discussions. The team was leaving soon for Brussels.

Several months later, Marti Waals, the Memisa program coordinator, asked me if I was willing to work with Memisa as a technical coordinator. I could not accept the offer because I was already working full time with the Congo MB conference and MBMS International. Still, I spent many hours helping Memisa design strategies suited to primary health care in the country. Because the Belgian doctor coordinating the program was leaving for another job, the Memisa board in Belgium, on Marti's recommendation, invited me to become their next national coordinator.

The most fascinating aspect of my job wasn't the technical part, but my encounter with my Belgian colleagues. In the town where the Memisa office was located, just outside Brussels, people tolerated outsiders speaking French, but preferred to speak English. I was shocked when I led our team to Antwerp for an international conference on sleeping sickness. The official language of the conference was English.

I continued working for Memisa until I left Congo in 1999.

CHAPTER 25

Joining Mennonite World Conference

1996–2009

I was still working for MBMS International when Larry Miller, general secretary of Mennonite World Conference, invited me in 1996 to work for MWC. My role was to lead a new project called Global Gift Sharing, established to set aside funds to encourage the sharing of gifts among churches. My colleague, Tim Lind, and I held the first Global Gift Sharing workshops in Africa in 1999. We continued these workshops in other parts of the world in early 2002.

The vision of Global Gift Sharing was to build and strengthen relationships among the global Mennonite, MB, and Brethren in Christ communities through the sharing of spiritual and material gifts and resources. By providing a modest structure through which this broad mandate could be nurtured, MWC hoped to work in a supportive way, while not duplicating efforts by other churches and church agencies.

Tim and I believed that the gifts God has given to every church member must be recognized and valued, and that the different kinds of suffering and needs experienced by the church calls for sharing these gifts.

Our vision put three biblical principles to work:

1. The church throughout the world is one. The diversity, differences, and the uniqueness of each part of the church are testimony to that oneness.

2. All gifts and resources come from and belong to God. All people, including the global church and its national conferences, local congregations, and individual members, are stewards of these gifts.

3. This stewardship involves a commitment to sharing, equality, and justice. God intends gifts to be used for and available to all of God's people.

More details on what we learned from the project can be found in a book that Tim and I wrote, *Sharing Gifts in the Global Family of Faith: One Church's Experiment* (Good Books).

I have long been sensitive to perceptions in the church about the "weak links" among us.

In 2001, I was attending MWC's executive committee meetings in Karlsruhe, Germany when I learned there is no such thing as weak link in a community of faith.

We were staying at Thomashof, a German Mennonite retreat center. Amid several days of meetings, our hosts had arranged for us to visit a few Mennonite historical sites in the region. On one outing, we were taken by bus to a church in Weierhof. When we arrived at the church, we realized that it was located on a hill and that I would have some difficulty reaching it.

I suggested that I would stay on the bus and that someone could tell me about it afterward.

"There is no way we can leave you down here," my friend Merle Good said. "We have to find a way of getting you up there. You need to hear the stories of this church together with all of us."

MWC treasurer Paul Quiring and Bishop Danisa from Zimbabwe agreed.

"Have a seat and we'll carry you up there," I heard someone behind me say. With that, I was lifted in a chair someone had borrowed and carried to the top of the stairs leading to the church. I was able to visit the church with everyone else and realized that some of the "weak links" in life are only as weak as we make them.

MWC's General Council, a body of about 125 leaders representing member churches, meets every three years. I was used to watching church leaders in Africa feel inferior when they met with North American or European church leaders because money was always part of the discussion. They always seemed afraid to express their feelings because they feared losing the little financial support they were getting. But at my first General Council meeting, I saw African, Asian, European, Latin American, and North American leaders discuss issues quite openly, in an atmosphere of mutuality. This was the only place I had witnessed all members of such a culturally varied group appearing to feel equal to everyone else around the table.

I grew up in a mission station where I was taught by missionaries and volunteers. And even though I'd worked for a mission agency as an adult, I was still naïve concerning the politics and impersonal "professionalization" of the church's and mission agencies' approach to mission.

At this global gathering of MWC's General Council, I learned a great deal about issues of power and control when it comes to the larger church and the people missionaries try to serve.

I've always believed that the job of mission agencies is to *assist* the church with the logistical and administrative aspects of mission. But the role of calling and sending people belongs to *the church*. These are spiritual functions. At the General Council meeting, I observed that many of those attending who represented North American mission agencies were trying to hold onto power, probably without even realizing it.

During the meeting, a series of recommendations about how churches around the world could work together mutually in mission had been made by a listening group designated by the General Council. The recommendations were widely accepted by the national church representatives on the Council. But then I observed leaders of several mission agencies attempting to manipulate the discussion, so that the decision about these ideas would be removed from the General Council members (representing the churches) and placed in the hands of a small group of North American agency leaders who seemed intent on defining the mission agenda. I heard comments such as, "Church leaders do not have the capacity and vision for mission. They don't understand all that is involved on the ground."

Members of the Council were asking MWC to create a neutral space of mutuality where the churches could come together to discuss issues related to mission or outreach beyond their own particular cultures. This idea had emerged simultaneously from church leaders in the room and also as a recommendation of the listening group. And when the idea was brought to the General Council formally for discussion, people were excited about such a possibility.

Unfortunately, one of the mission agency leaders was moderating the discussion that day. Someone moved that the General Council approve the recommendation. I watched four or five of the agency leaders, accustomed to being movers and shakers, consult each other as the General Council members were discussing.

And then the moderator proposed that it would not be appropriate for the General Council to approve this recommendation from the listening group. Instead, a small commission should be established by MWC and the Council of International Ministries (the network of mission agencies), the two bodies that had organized the consultation, to decide what the next steps should be. I was shocked!

I later asked a couple of church leaders from Africa why they went along with the moderator's suggestion when they knew that was not the direction they wanted to take. "They have the money," they said. "We must agree with them. Otherwise, where will we get the money for our work?" Money was talking loud and clear again.

Ironically, when representatives of the national churches were asked to choose people to serve on the leadership committee of the Global Anabaptist Mission Fellowship, a new international body that was formed during the Council meeting, they did not select anyone who had followed the direction of the North American mission agency leaders. Several years later, the Mission Fellowship leadership asked to become part of Mennonite World Conference's global network, thereby coming under the umbrella of the *church*.

When I was invited in 2002 to join MWC's fulltime staff as associate general secretary, I accepted, joining Larry Miller and Ray Brubacher on the executive staff. I was still pondering the lessons I'd learned at my first General Council meeting when I attended a similar gathering in Bulawayo, Zimbabwe, in 2003. With Mennonites in attendance from around the world, I became impressed by what seemed like a quilt or mosaic of people and nations. During worship, I felt a sense of oneness with everyone. The music, sung in several languages, reinforced feeling.

In 2003, I traveled to Bulawayo for the MWC global assembly. Zimbabwe's political and economic situation was tense and some felt it foolish to hold the assembly in such a place, and that it would only support a corrupt political regime. As an African, I felt strongly that we should go where our brothers and sisters needed us most.

Worshipping with nearly 7,000 people in Bulawayo was the best experience of my life. Being in a country where our brothers and sisters were suffering for their beliefs was the best Christian testimony I could imagine. I still return to Zimbabwe each year to work with women and orphans affected by the HIV/AIDS pandemic.

The author in his Fresno, California, home office in 2007.

Working with MWC has given me an opportunity to become more aware of the incredible number of gifted people in each member church. Many efforts are being made to connect churches in new ways, and I have become aware of the miserable conditions under which many churches work. I have been impressed to learn that besides Mennonite and Brethren in Christ churches in North America, Europe, and a few in Asia and Latin America, all the other Mennonite and Brethren in Christ churches are economically very poor. In countries with little economic power, members of these churches tend to be at the bottom of the economic ladder.

Congo is home to more than a quarter of all the Mennonites in the world. I remembered the women I met in eastern Congo who were fighting for survival because they felt they had lost their womanhood to the brutal sexual violence they experienced during the war there. Militia groups and soldiers from Congo and neighboring countries who were committing these atrocities felt like little gods because they thought they would never face justice for what they had done.

We seem to be forging new ways of relating to one another and yet brutal violence and economic disparities still interfere.

CHAPTER 26

Instilling Order Amid Chaos

1940s-1960s, 1980s-1990s

I grew up believing laws were developed to foster order in society. Our Chokwe culture also had its own value system that provided a social framework. We didn't have written laws, but we had rules to abide by. I was taught not to hand something to someone older with my left hand. You stood up if you were sitting when an elder walked into a room. When you reached adolescence, you were expected to learn to provide for your future family. Boys were separated from girls during adolescence, and social roles became more defined. A young man who could not fish, hunt, or work in the field had a hard time finding a family to give him a daughter for a wife. The same was true for a young woman who didn't know how to cook or take care of small family chores.

Europeans introduced other practices, among them our current police and military systems. Things were different in Kajiji, where everything was built around the church and everyone knew each other. When there were conflicts or other social issues to address, the church elders dealt with them instead of going before the authorities at the nearby government post.

The government post in later years was administered by people we all knew and who were familiar with many of the local practices. The first local government chief was Papa Louis Kafusa. He was a Protestant and was related to us on our mother's side. Many times on Sunday, he and his family walked the two miles that separated Kajiji from the government post to attend church. I remember them stopping at our house for a meal or a cup of coffee before going home. He also came to talk with my dad about various government affairs or for counsel about something that had been disturbing him. Papa Louis died suddenly one evening after hosting a large group at his house. According to rumors, the chief of the local clan had given Papa Louis a vase with some sort of protective liquid in it. He was supposed to check it every day and no women were supposed to see into the vase. The day he saw blood inside the vase meant the end of his life had arrived. I understood that on the evening in question, after all his guests had left, Kafusa went to check the vase and noticed it was full of blood. He told his wife he wasn't going to live much longer, and that night he died.

He was replaced by Papa Dingenu, who also was a friend of my family. My mother told me how she took care of their son when Mama Dingenu was hospitalized for several days. Because their son was the same age as my brother, Tshinabu, who was still being breastfed, my mother just added another baby to be fed with her milk until the child's mother was released from the hospital.

Other dignitaries came to our house as well, so we got to know many of them by helping our parents entertain them. This is how we learned not to be afraid of government officials or policemen. The police knew members of our family would report them if they harassed us, but it was a different story for the soldiers.

Everyone in Kajiji feared the government soldiers. I remember the first time soldiers came to Kajiji. We were in church on a Sunday morning. Someone walked to the front of the sanctuary and murmured something in my dad's ear. My father turned and whispered something to the other people on the platform. Before long, the whole church was empty.

People were running in the direction of the government post, where violence was brewing. I asked my mother what was going on.

"A young boy your age was run over and killed by a Belgian businessman," she told us. The local government leaders informed the military base at Kahemba that the people there were ready to kill the businessman. Soon, a truck full of soldiers, blacks and whites, arrived in Kajiji to search for the riot instigators. Several young people were arrested, beaten, and taken to Kahemba.

Because Kajiji was built around an Anabaptist church, our young people were discouraged from joining the army. I knew only two soldiers during my whole childhood who were from the villages near us. When they were visiting their families, however, they sometimes stayed in our home.

In the 1960s, following Congo's independence from Belgium, a civil war ravaged the country. President Mobutu took over in a bloodless coup in 1965. For a short time, he brought peace and tranquility. However, before long, he became as greedy as the Belgian leaders before him. Together with his cronies, he started to hoard national resources and let everyone starve. Mobutu combined the military and the police under a ministry of defense, thus removing the police from the civilian ministry of interior. At first it seemed like this was for greater efficiency, but it didn't take long to realize it was a move toward control and self-preservation.

As a public health professional, travel was an integral part of my work. I traveled to villages for maternal and child health clinics. I went to Kikwit and Kinshasa for meetings and conferences, and to purchase medicine, supplies, and other goods we needed. I also traveled regularly to the United States, Canada, France, Switzerland, Belgium, and Angola for meetings and conferences. Each trip made me realize the depth of the lawlessness in my country.

The worse the economic situation became, the meaner the police, the military, and the immigration officers became. Friends from other parts of the world asked me how one could live and work in such a place, where those who were meant to help the people had become terrorists, and law and order were suspended.

CHAPTER 27

Roadblocks

1980s–1990s, 2000–2003

While working on the MWC Global Gift Sharing Project, my colleague, Tim Lind, and I were traveling in a rented car from Victoria Falls in Zimbabwe to Choma in Zambia. A little more than an hour after crossing the Zambian border, we were stopped at a roadblock.

"Can I see your driver's license and the vehicle documents?" the policeman asked. Tim showed him the papers he requested, including the additional insurance we had purchased at the border. The policeman stood by the car for awhile, then asked us if we had a triangle.

"What is a triangle?" I asked the policeman.

"You don't know what a triangle is?" he said. "It is a reflector you put next to your vehicle to warn other drivers in case your car breaks down. It is the law in Zambia. You cannot drive without it."

Tim got out, looked in the trunk and under the seats, but the triangle was nowhere to be found. "It seems like we don't have one in this car, so what do we do?" I asked.

"You must pay a fine for not having one," he replied.

Tim and I looked at each other, and I shook my head to indicate that we were not going to pay anything. We asked him to tell his supervisor that we were foreigners, that our car was a rental, and that we didn't feel responsible for not having it in the car. While he was gone, we talked about how this roadblock reminded us so much of what we used to experience on the roads in Congo.

He returned a few minutes later to inform us that his supervisor said we must pay the fine. I asked the policeman to come to my side of the car because I wanted to ask him a question.

"What is the role of policemen?" I asked. Before he had the chance to answer, I asked him if policemen weren't supposed to educate the public about the law. He went back to his supervisor for a few minutes. They must have realized we weren't going to give them any money, so when he came back, he lifted the barricade and wished us a good trip. We laughed all the way to Choma as we thought about the good old days of roadblocks in Congo.

In Congo, roadblocks were fascinating, amusing, angering, challenging, and frustrating. They could pop up anywhere without warning. Someone always seemed to find an excellent reason to erect one. Worst was the road between Kikwit and Kinshasa. After so much travel among Kajiji, Kikwit, and Kinshasa by road, I started to recognize some of the officials managing the roadblocks. Unfortunately, the officers from Kahemba, Kikwit, and Kinshasa seldom kept the same soldiers on the same roadblocks for very long. Furthermore, there was no guarantee that roadblocks would always be in the same place, except in strategic locations such as bridges.

The regular procedure was for the soldiers or policemen to ask for the vehicle registration and insurance papers. Next they asked for identification documents for all the passengers. We knew the name of the game, so we never traveled with more than the number of people our vehicle was insured for. We also made sure everyone in the vehicle had his or her official traveling papers, including personal ID and a letter from their employers or spouses. Because I worked for the church, then later with Memisa, I made sure I wrote a travel authorization for staff traveling with me. Occasionally, a policeman pulled a fast one, even when all the documents were in order.

"Do you have your baptism card?" or "Where is your marriage license?" one of them might ask.

We then had two options, either to give them a few pennies or to just sit in the vehicle and wait for them to get tired of us and lift the barricade to let us go. As often as possible, we chose the latter.

With time, some of them started to recognize our vehicles, so they inquired about Bibles or any kind of Christian literature we might be carrying. I often carried extra bread, small packages of aspirin, and pocket-size New Testaments. As soon as we got to familiar roadblocks, we stopped.

"How are you guys doing?" I asked. "Are you keeping everybody safe on the road these days? Here is some bread and some aspirin we brought you."

Every so often, we gave them a tin of sardines or corned beef, because sometimes they really looked miserable.

I was told of a Congolese law that prohibited people from taking pictures of bridges, airports, and military barracks. I could understand not photographing the military barracks, but the airport and the bridges didn't make sense to me. I took pictures anywhere I wanted.

Roadblocks were not only in rural locations. Many of them were erected in the middle of town or at the city limits. In 1993, while we were living in Kikwit, a friend of ours, Dr. Paul Bottom, a physician from Nebraska, spent a couple of weeks in Kajiji, then joined us to work at our small clinic in Kikwit. Keji, our driver, dropped him off at the clinic in the morning, then picked him up at the end of the day. To get to the clinic, one had to cross a bridge on a small stream that fed into the bigger Kwilu River. A roadblock often was established between these bridges.

There were always two groups of guards—military police and traffic policemen. The day Paul was to leave for Kinshasa on an MAF plane, he went to work at the clinic in the morning. His flight was scheduled for the afternoon, so we agreed he could work until noon. Then someone would bring him on a motorcycle to my office, and we would drive to the airport. In the meantime, I kept contact by short-wave radio with the MAF pilot. The routine was that I provided them weather information, and they gave me their estimated time of arrival. One of the pilots and his family lived at Vanga, a Baptist mission station just a few minutes' flight to Kikwit. I usually waited for him to take off before we drove to the airport.

I waited for Paul to arrive in my office at noon, but he didn't show up. Our receptionist knocked at my door in a panic and informed me that the clinic administrator looked very scared and wanted to see me urgently.

"Dr. Bottom has been stopped by the soldiers and the policemen guarding the bridge, and they won't let him go," he told me. "He is being accused of taking pictures of two bridges and of women bathing in the river."

"That's ridiculous," I responded.

I called up Keji and we headed for the bridge. Paul was still waiting there. They didn't harass him, but they had taken away his camera. I asked the soldiers and the policemen what the matter was.

"You know it is against the law to take pictures of bridges, and this man also has been taking pictures of women in the river," one of them said.

"I don't believe you because I know this man," I said. "This is not his first time in our country. He is not the kind who would dishonor our people. Our health-care system has fallen apart, and we invite him regularly to come and help us. He comes on his own, and we don't pay him anything for all the services he renders for our people. I suggest that you give him his camera, and I will come later to deal with you."

After a few minutes of silence, the team leader handed me the camera and told me to come back later so we could talk. I knew he was expecting a bribe and I also knew that he wasn't going to get it.

We drove Paul to the airport, and, soon after he was gone, I asked Keji to take me back to the bridge where the same team of soldiers and policemen were on duty.

"Where is the white man?" the team leader asked me.

"He is gone. He just left for Kinshasa a few minutes ago," I informed them.

"And the camera? Where is it?" he asked me. "I gave it back to Dr. Bottom, and he took it with him. As I just told you, he left a few minutes ago for Kinshasa, and he is leaving this evening for the USA."

They all got very angry with me. I suggested they arrest me because I had made it possible for Paul to leave Kikwit. One of them talked about how they lacked the evidence because Paul, the guilty party, had taken the camera with him, and they had nothing to show for the "crime" that had been committed.

They were all quiet for a moment. Then I asked them what they wanted to do next. I suggested they take me to the police headquarters or report me to their battalion. I also suggested this might constitute a case of treason, so it might be a good idea to go directly to their bosses rather than wasting our time under the sun.

I was given a chair while the policemen and the soldiers gathered in a corner and got into a heated discussion. Keji, my driver, said I had created a problem for these soldiers and policemen.

"What is the problem?" I asked Keji.

A couple of the soldiers finally realized who I was and knew my role in the community and my relationship with the local leaders. They also knew I was a friend of the head general of the Congolese 5th Military Region, and that the general would be angry if he heard I had been detained. Consequently, they were trying to find a way to let me go while saving face.

"You can go. Just know that what you did was wrong," the team leader told me.

I refused to leave. Finally, the leaders told me I should remember that Congolese soldiers like to deal with tough guys like me.

"Let's call it even," he concluded. We left and went home. Three weeks later, four of them came to my office to ask forgiveness for the way they had treated me.

More Travel Adventures

1990s, 2000–2003

Having a Congolese passport taught me many lessons about immigration officers and foreign consulate personnel. I was naïve to believe that all one needed when applying for a visa was a valid passport. I had assumed that securing a visa was a fair game, no matter where you were from, and that you always could trust immigration officials.

While I was working for Mennonite World Conference, Tim Lind and I needed to travel to Colombia and Guatemala. Because of my Congolese passport, even though I was living in California as a resident alien, I still needed visas to enter both countries. Both had consular offices in San Francisco, and I was told I could get a visa for Guatemala the same day if I arrived in the office before noon. As for Colombia, because I was traveling on a Congolese passport, their law required a five-day wait.

The author with his wife, Linda, near the Congo River in 1996.

It took less than an hour to get a visa for Guatemala. I then took a taxi and rushed to the Colombian consulate, where I was well received by a young woman working at the front desk. She took my papers and went to a back room, where she gave them to another of her colleagues.

"Good morning, Mr. Tshimika," that person said. "It looks like you have all the documents you need. After we process your visa, we can either mail you the passport or you can pick it up in five days."

"That's too long," I said. "Can't you grant the visa today so I won't have to come back again?"

"Sorry, with your Congolese passport we need to make a background check before we decide if you can be granted a visa," he told me.

I told the gentleman I thought he could make an exception if he wanted to. I told him how it took less than an hour to be granted the Guatemalan visa and thought Colombians could do better than that. While we were talking, the consul joined us and asked about the situation in Congo. I told them about the region of Congo where I come from. I said I had a special interest in Colombia because of its indigenous Choko people.

"I come from the Chokwe tribe in Congo but my dad was born in Angola," I said. "I have always wondered if the Choko from Colombia are not among our people who were brought to the Americas and the Caribbean from Angola and Congo."

The consul shared with me about his friends among the Chokos, gave me his card, and asked me to contact him whenever I needed help visiting the region.

"Go ahead and stamp his passport, and I will sign so he can have his visa today," the consul told the gentleman who had my papers.

I need a visa for almost all the countries I visit when I travel internationally. In Europe, France became a real thorn in my flesh. Applying for a visa to enter or simply to pass through could be full of frustration, anger, paradox, and surprises. The environment of the French consulate sections in Kinshasa and San Francisco don't make you feel welcome, either. In Kinshasa, as in San Francisco, you have to stand in line outside the building for a long time. It doesn't make any difference if you are physically fit or disabled. And in Kinshasa, whenever noon arrives, the visa office closes, no matter how long you have been waiting, even under the very hot Central African sun.

Once, when I wanted to visit my brother and his family before continuing to Kinshasa, I went to San Francisco to apply for a visa for France. Five days later, I received the visa. I had spent three days with my brother in Paris when violence erupted in Congo Brazzaville the day before I was supposed to leave Paris. All the flights to Brazzaville were cancelled. Finally, three days later, I was able to fly in. But this wasn't the end of the trouble. A few days before leaving Kinshasa, I went to reconfirm my flight. I was told I needed to check again with the French consulate regarding my visa status before I could travel on Air France through Paris.

"We cannot let you travel on this flight," a young woman at the consulate said.

"Why not?" I asked.

She said I could not pass through two European countries that were party to the Schengen Agreement, which was meant to expedite travel among different nations in Europe.

"I just came through Paris not too long ago," I said. "I even stayed a couple more days due to fighting in Brazzaville, so why is it hard to go back through Paris again? Do you know that I am only going through the airport and that I am not even staying in France?"

"I know, but there is nothing I can really do," she said. "It is the law."

I asked to see the consul, and she agreed to make an appointment for me. In the meantime, I went to consult with friends who were connected with the Belgian Embassy in

Kinshasa. I discovered that I was classified as an "undesirable in France."

I arrived early for my appointment with the consul. He received me well, and I explained that I was just going through Paris and that they didn't have to worry about me staying in the country and becoming a burden on their government.

"I am sorry. The order is from Paris," he insisted.

As we talked, I noticed that I was becoming impatient and angry. I began to tell him about how I didn't want to be in that stupid country of theirs. I told him that I had a good job and residency status in the United States, so why would I forfeit all that to live in France, a country I didn't even like?

"What can I do to get a visa for France?" I asked. "If I am an undesirable, then what is it going to take for me to become desirable in your country? What made me undesirable to start with?"

"They don't have to tell you," he finally explained. "Why don't you write me an official letter explaining your professional and residency situation, and I'll try to help you."

He seemed to be a kind man. I agreed to write a letter to the consul, and he said he would grant me a visa for the airport while he waited for my letter. I contacted several Belgian friends, and they suggested I write the ambassador instead, with copies to the consul and other European Union embassies in Kinshasa.

In my letter, I included information regarding my residency status in the United States, indicating that I was working for a U.S.-based organization, that my wife was American, and that French law permitted me to travel through France without a transit visa unless I wanted to leave the airport. I concluded by suggesting they open a legal case against me if I were so undesirable in France. I never received an answer from the ambassador or the consul. Instead, my visa was granted, and I left for Fresno. Afterward, I still had to wait five days for a visa as "required" by law, but it was no longer an issue of being undesirable.

Why was I undesirable in France? I had never been expelled from any country, never been in jail, and never been taken to court. I used to travel to Europe regularly. I went annually to Belgium for Memisa meetings and didn't have any problem with the law, immigration, or customs. One day, while visiting with Howard and Irene Loewen in Fresno, I shared with them about the difficulty I had been having with the French authorities. Irene asked me to try to think about anything I could have said or done that might be related to their government.

"Oh, yes!" I exclaimed. "I think I have an idea."

It all started after a shopping trip to Kinshasa, while we lived in Kikwit. When we arrived back in Kikwit, people were surprised that we had made it. Immediately after we left Kinshasa, a riot had broken out. The soldiers dispersed people by shooting into the air. During the violence, the French ambassador was killed by a stray bullet. The ambassador's death became a subject of much discussion because there was a small French community in Kikwit. With several friends, we tried to provide support for them as they mourned the loss of their representative in Congo.

The ambassador's death seemed very suspicious to most of us, and we encouraged several nuns and priests from the French community in Kikwit to write a letter to authorities in France to complain about the lack of a solid investigation. The letter also included comments about French President Francois Mitterrand's support for President Mobutu while the Congolese were starving. Six of us signed the letter as friends of the Kikwit French community. The letter was dropped on President Mitterrand's desk by one of the nun's cousins, a member of the French parliament. In addition, the letter was sent to all the European Union members with embassies in Kinshasa, most major European newspapers, and TV and radio stations.

The French government didn't appreciate the letter and, furthermore, they didn't like it having such a wide distribution. My simple act of signing this letter was what had made me so "undesirable" to the French government.

CHAPTER 29

Returning Home

2005

If its numbers were considered significant, the current war in Congo would be on the front pages of all the world's newspapers. Millions of people are not aware of what is going on in Congo, or how this disinterest might appear from the Congolese perspective.

In August 2004, I went to Strasbourg, France, for Mennonite World Conference meetings, then visited my sister-in-law and her three children in Paris before returning to California. Our youngest daughter, Patience, was traveling with me. In Frankfurt, Germany, as soon as we had settled into our seats for the long flight back to San Francisco, I started thinking about a trip I would make to Congo in January 2005.

This would be my first personal trip back since my family had moved to Fresno in August 1999. Sonja Heinrichs, together with Dalton Reimer, my former college professor from Fresno, and Ray Dirks, a professional artist and photographer from Winnipeg, Manitoba, accompanied me on the journey. This was to be Sonja's first trip to Africa. Almost 30 years before, I had promised to show her my homeland.

Thinking about the trip brought back many sad memories, knowing that my immediate family was nearly all gone. I had only two siblings left out of a family of nine children. Both my parents were now dead, and many of my childhood friends had died either due to AIDS or a lack of access to health care. The political and economic situation was worse than I had ever known. The country had been at war for more than

With American "sister" Sonja Heinrichs in the Kajiji, Congo, church in 2005.

five years. Traveling across the country was challenging, but I was determined to visit my home village.

We traveled to Kinshasa in January 2005. The Congolese have a strong will to live, no matter their circumstances. Doctors, nurses, teachers, and government officials continued to work with the limited resources available to them. Women and children stood on every street corner, selling goods to help feed their families and pay school fees.

Dr. Kalumuna is a physician I knew when we lived in Kinshasa. We attended the same church. He felt a strong call to move back to his home of origin in Bukavu. When war started again in 1998, Dr. Kalumuna was caught in the crossfire and ended up living in the Bukavu hospital for a week, taking care of the sick and wounded. During that week, he didn't know what had happened to his family. He was later reunited with them, but only after many agonizing days. When I asked him why he was still in Bukavu, given all he had gone through, he immediately said that he felt God's unchanging call to go to Bukavu. Dr. Kalumuna represented the spirit of many other Congolese who have spent their lives serving others under similar conditions.

In Kinshasa, we met Jackie, a single woman in her late 30s. Jackie's passion is adopting children orphaned by AIDS or abandoned in local hospitals. She had 13 children, ages 3 to 12, living with her. As far as she was concerned, these were her children. When I asked how long she planned to keep these children, she seemed puzzled. "Do you have children, Dr. Pakisa?" she asked me. "How long do you plan to keep them?" I saw her point. The children had a home. Their basic needs were being met. Jackie had started a small business making yogurt to help with her family's income. Jackie didn't wait for manna to drop from heaven. She worked with what she had or could create. Every once in a while friends lent her a helping hand.

In Congo, we also found a country where about four million people have died since the outbreak of the latest civil war in 1996, many from preventable diseases. In addition, more than two million people are internally displaced, with more than 50 percent in the eastern part of the country. More than a million of these displaced people have received no outside assistance. In speaking with government and civil leaders, we learned that at least 18.5 million people had no access to formal health care, and 16 million people had critical food needs. Only 2,056 doctors remained in the country for a population of about 50 million, and 930 of these physicians were in Kinshasa.

For many people around the world, these are just statistics. For me, these are the cruel realities of life. These figures represent my brothers and sisters, nephews and nieces, friends I went to school with, and future leaders of the country. Almost 24 hours after we arrived in Kinshasa, we were confronted by the death of a four-year-old girl in a clinic we were visiting. The little girl, the daughter of a pastor, was anemic, and her skin was very pale when we saw her. She needed a blood transfusion, but there was none to give her. My friend, Pascal, who was driving us around, took the mother and child to a larger hospital nearby. Three hours later, she died. The child's mother and I had grown up together. Our parents had been lifelong friends. The same scene repeated itself in Kajiji, my hometown. Soon after our arrival, we received news of the death of one of my favorite cousins about 60 miles away. She had died of AIDS that morning.

Visiting each day with friends, professional colleagues, and leaders, we found a country where people feel isolated and forgotten by the rest of the world. That feeling was best expressed by someone in eastern Congo in a report by Amnesty International: "I am convinced now ... that the lives of Congolese people no longer mean anything to anybody. Not to those who kill us like flies, our brothers who help kill us, or those you call the international community. ... Even God does not listen to our prayers anymore."

We also found a country where representatives of international aid organizations feel frustrated. Oxfam criticized the international community for ignoring Congo. When they compared the international community's response in Kosovo, they pointed out that "in 1999, donor governments gave just $8 per person in [Congo], while providing $207 per person in response to the [United Nations] appeal for the former Yugoslavia. While it is clear that both regions have significant needs, there is little commitment to *universal* entitlement to humanitarian assistance."

Oxfam also noted that "the international community is essentially ignoring what has been deemed 'Africa's first world war.' [Congo] remains a forgotten emergency."

In Kinshasa, we discovered schools without places for children to sit. Women from the community had transformed several classrooms into kitchens when children were not present. Kikwit, a city of 500,000 people, was no different. Today, many schools are without walls. It frightened us to think about what happens to children in this city.

In Kajiji, we found crowded schools and students without access to books or school supplies. We found only three sewing machines for 120 students in a girls' training school, where they are supposed to learn about home economics and sewing. The hospital pharmacy was empty, and hospital beds were without mattresses and linens.

In the hospital, we discovered a little boy sitting in his mother's lap outside the pediatric ward. For someone unfamiliar with tropical diseases, his skin looked like third-degree burns. He was suffering from severe malnutrition, and yet the hospital couldn't afford to buy milk to feed him. It doesn't make any difference how the country arrived where it was. People created in God's image were dying unnecessarily, and those still alive were feeling isolated and abandoned.

Children in hospital beds in Kajiji hospital in 2005.

I couldn't help but cry each day as I listened and saw what was happening to this beautiful country and its people. Each morning, I contemplated this as I sat on the veranda of the house where we were staying and watched the fog rise from the valley. Singing gospel songs on Sunday morning in church was comforting, but it didn't take away the pain I was feeling. But as soon as I returned to visiting with friends, local chiefs, and hard-working women whose sense of hope was slipping away, my heart broke once again.

We now found soldiers roaming the countryside, even though this region wasn't affected directly by war. These soldiers were actually little more than children carrying guns. I wondered how government leaders could do such a thing to my people. We listened with great sadness as a local chief spoke about the pain these young soldiers caused in the area, including rape, extortion, stealing, and forced labor. There was nothing he could do because they were out of his control.

He wanted to promote development in the region and require accountability of all government employees under his supervision, but he felt his hands were tied. Two months later, we received news that he had died suddenly.

How is it that even my own denomination back in North America recognizes that the Congo church membership is the largest within our family of faith and yet has never considered the situation in Congo a priority? Is this an issue of racism or world view? Why is it that the situation in my country is still ignored by so many, even though more people are dying in Congo than died during the Rwandan genocide of the mid-1990s?

Maybe Martin Luther King Jr. was right when he challenged people to develop a different world view. The world in which we live is geographically one, he said. Dr. King said we must all learn to live together as brothers and sisters or perish together as fools.

After I got back to Fresno, I continued to ponder what we had seen, heard, smelled, and touched, and I tried to figure out how to respond. I still heard the voices calling me like an African drum toward a dance that brought peace and reconciliation, hope for the future for schoolchildren, basic medicine to hospitals, and good governance by all in power.

I also continued to hear the author Henri Nouwen calling and reminding me, together with all my friends in a loud voice, saying, "Our faithfulness will depend on our willingness to go where there is brokenness, loneliness, and human need."

CHAPTER 30

A House of Hope

2002–2009

The past few years, I have been helping a group of women in eastern Congo share their stories of sexual abuse and other violence with the rest of the world.

I first met these women in 2006. I had gone to visit the Kalumuna family in Bukavu following several years of unrest in the region. I also visited a small Mennonite church there and connected with COPARE, a consortium of local NGOs with a peacebuilding agenda. I was accompanied by Dalton Reimer, Pascal Kulungu, and Serge Tshinyama.

While in Bukavu, I asked Yvette Kalumuna if we could visit the Panzi hospital, which cares for women who experienced often severe sexual violence during the years of fighting in the region. I had read of them in *Ms.* magazine, which my friend, Dr. Gail Newel, had given me.

"Why do you want to go to Panzi hospital?" Yvette asked. "That's where all the funding is going, but do you know where all these women come from? Nobody wants to go to the villages in the Walungu district where they come from. You know that the U.N. considers the Walungu region to be a red zone with grave health risks."

I wasn't afraid, so we decided to visit the hospital and one of the villages. It had rained overnight and the road was very slippery. We drove slowly through very beautiful green mountains where men and women were working. This region produced the best tea and coffee in the country. We used to buy cheese, potatoes, and green peas from Kivu before the war started. Due to the war, many people were afraid to work in their fields. So it was good to observe renewed agricultural activities as we drove from village to village. There were many soldiers along the road, but they didn't disturb us.

We arrived at the hospital, where we were welcomed by Dr. John and his team. Our visit at the hospital was short. Dr. John showed us around, then offered to accompany us to the village an hour away. There, we were welcomed by a group of almost 70 women. Yvette introduced the women, then asked me to say something. What do you say to a group of women who have been sexually violated? They had been abused by men like me, so why should they listen? I decided to share with them about my own pain of losing my mother and sister because of greedy leaders and the consequences of war. The women looked sad and felt sympathy for me. I told them I couldn't comprehend what they had gone through, but said I had brought my friends to assure them that we wouldn't forget them.

Yvette asked if they had anything to say in response, and their stories changed my life. One after another, these women told of how they had been kidnapped and raped, sometimes in front of their spouses and children. One young woman spoke of the ordeal she had endured in the mountains with her kidnappers. She was raped multiple times and became pregnant. But three months later, she was shot while trying to escape and lost her baby. She bled from her wound and retained her placenta for 10 days. In the meantime, she was moved from one militia to another until two different groups began to fight over whose woman she was. By some miracle, she was released and left in the hands of the local Red Cross.

I sobbed as I listened to these women, who ranged in age from their teens to their 60s. I saw in them my aunts, sisters, nieces, and my own daughters. They pleaded with us to share their stories with the world. We promised to come back, and we did in January 2007.

Many years earlier, after my mother's death, I had promised I would do everything I could to assist other women. As a result, I founded an NGO called the Mama Makeka House of Hope, in honor of my mother, with the mission of sharing a sense of hope to the under-served and the marginalized.

In January 2008, several friends, including my former college professor, Dalton Reimer, Dr. Gail Newel, Sarah Hagey, my niece, Rebekah, and I went back to Walungu. We went back with three concrete commitments to:

The author the last time he saw his mother, Rebekah, in Congo in 2001.

1. Collaborate with the Walungu Health Zone to assist with physical and emotional healing, and empowerment opportunities for women who have experienced sexual violence. Specifically, we would offer peer counseling training in trauma healing; management training and seed funding for a micro-credit program; sewing machines, supplies, and training for an income-generation program; and supplies and training for doctors specializing in obstetrics surgery at the Walungu hospital.

2. Develop a documentary project that would focus on women of the Walungu region who have been victims of sexual violence.

3. Support initiatives that promote security in the Walungu region by building relationships with grassroots peace and reconciliation groups in South Kivu. Specifically, we would participate in collecting and exchanging weapons for bicycles or tin roofing. Weapons would be melted down and transformed into agricultural tools.

∼

In 2006, Congo held its first democratic election in 46 years. I was an international observer for this election which I never thought I would see. Today, Congo is a country under reconstruction after more than 30 years of dictatorship and seven years of war and conflict. There is a sense of optimism among the Congolese people and a strong desire to rebuild the country on a new and strong foundation. One gets a feeling of a new era beginning in this large and potentially rich nation.

The optimism and sense of renaissance in Congo is a challenge especially for those of us around the world who still have strong roots there. We can no longer just complain about how terrible or miserable things had been in the past, but we must bring the building blocks that are needed to rebuild Congo, no matter how small these blocks might appear. I feel a sense of urgency and a commitment to engage, capture the opportunities, and walk alongside those already involved in recreating my homeland.

Home:
A Place for People
Seeking Refuge

Recently, as I often do, I was speaking about the current situation in Congo when a listener asked me, "Are you ever afraid of anything in your life?" I had to think for awhile before I answered. The news about the region in the international media is usually about the abduction and rape of women and internally displaced people. We're shown images of women and children in displacement camps, where many suffer from tropical diseases. The people in the audience who were familiar with the region found it difficult to understand how I could travel there without fearing for my own safety.

"I think my biggest fear is not being involved in the lives of other people, especially when I know I can be a voice for them," I finally replied.

I believe a person's home should also be a place of refuge for those who need it. It must be a safe sanctuary for the family who lives there, but also for others from the community, and for sojourners. As a child in Congo, I remember a mob of about 40 people chasing a young man who had been involved in a fight with another man. The young man had suffered a head injury, and his family and friends decided they would kill his opponent. I remember the young man running toward our house. My father said to let him in, even though this could have put our family in danger.

I am not sure if my dad was afraid, but I remember him telling the mob to calm down and go back home. He said he would work with the perpetrator and, when appropriate, would call for a meeting with the village elders. Did my parents think twice about being a voice or providing a sanctuary for someone in danger? It didn't seem so. I guess that is where it all began for me.

Linda and I moved to Kinshasa in 1994 from Kikwit, after I became director for Africa for the MB mission agency. We were among six families who started a French MB congregation in Kinshasa. Our goal was to provide a church where people from the international community felt at home. Many people from African embassies in Kinshasa began to worship with us. Several of the women from the congregation also began reaching out to refugees from other African countries.

The refugee situation in Africa is fascinating. For many years, one could find Congolese who were refugees in Angola, the Central African Republic, Uganda, Rwanda, Sudan, Tanzania, and Zambia. In turn, these same countries also had refugees in Congo. Several refugees were part of our congregation.

We first met Emmanuel, who came from a nearby country (that I should not name for his own safety), one Sunday morning. When he decided to join the church, he began to receive death threats from his old friends and former religious community. They tried several times to run him over while he was riding his bicycle. As the threats grew, we offered him a room in our home. We learned to love him, and he became a big brother to our children.

Emmanuel had been involved in his country's student movement and had been very angry with the oppressive regime there. As a result, he sought refuge in Congo, and we hosted him for more than a year until he found a permanent home in Canada. With Canadian citizenship, he can now travel back to his home country without fear of being killed, although he has to steer clear of those who knew him before and see him through the eyes of the past.

Our senior pastor had worked for several years in a neighboring country, where he taught at a theological school after completing his doctoral studies in southern California. Through the congregation he was attending then, he began a Bible study in the presidential palace. The president's brother attended the same church with our pastor, and that's where he also met John (not his real name), a young officer trained in a prestigious military school.

John was the president's nephew and a wonderful singer and sang in the church choir. He came to Kinshasa after someone saved his life by helping him escape from one of the most notorious prisons in Africa. Soon, however, some people from his embassy who were attending our church informed their superiors about his presence in our church. His life in danger once again, we invited him to live with us.

We had wonderful conversations each evening after supper. With John and Emmanuel around the table, we spent hours hearing their stories of heroism, pain, and courage. I once asked John why the president of his country wanted his head so badly. He said he wasn't afraid in Congo while President Mobutu was in power because he had been his uncle's friend. When President Kabila took power, he signed an agreement with the neighboring presidents to turn over many of Mobutu's collaborators. John was on the top of the list. However, President Kabila could not find enough reason to arrest John and send him home.

When John had been in prison, a guard helped him one Sunday afternoon. He told John he had been given poison to kill him, but that he could not do it. When John asked him why he didn't just kill him to put him out of his misery, he told him that once John had saved him from major embarrassment when his wife was pregnant. The guard had not saved money for the child's arrival, so he didn't have food or clothes for his wife and the baby. After the baby was born, John had purchased clothes and food, and also gave them cash so they would have enough money to organize a reception for their family and friends. "How could I kill someone who did so much good for me?" the guard asked him.

I instructed everyone in our home to be alert for anyone looking for John while he continued to take refuge with us. All this changed, though, one Christmas Day. We had invited many friends to join us in the afternoon for a meal. A group from more than eight nations ate together that afternoon when three people walked into our yard. John was sitting next to me when these people came, and he turned to me and said, "I think it's over for me." I asked him to go inside the house. I invited these three men to come over and asked how I could assist them.

"We are from the presidential security office, and we came to talk with you because we have been told that you are hosting three people who are illegally in this country," the team leader said. "One of them is a son of a former dictator of our neighboring country."

"There is some truth in what you are saying, but I am surprised that you come from the presidential security system and yet you don't have accurate information," I said. "I have three people from other countries living with me, but each one of them has his regular papers." I went on to tell them that the person alleged to be the son of a former dictator actually wasn't such a person at all.

I told them to inform their superiors that there were three foreigners living with my family and that no one would touch them as long as I was alive. Furthermore, I told them that I knew they were after John, but that Congo is a place for refuge and people shouldn't be deported to another country where they would be killed. I also asked them to tell President Kabila himself to remember that he spent many years in exile in Tanzania before returning to get rid of Mobutu.

The team leader didn't know how to respond. He said he was a Christian and that I had put him in a difficult situation. I told him to just report what I had said and what they had seen. Then we invited them to join us for our meal, and they did. Before leaving, the team leader suggested I do everything I could to get John out of the country immediately.

We worked hard to find ways to get John out of Congo. Finally, through friends in Kinshasa, we were able to get John the documents and ticket he needed to leave. Unfortunately, I could not accompany him to the airport because it would have attracted too much attention and could have endangered us both.

After John left, I learned that a young man from my congregation had been paid $100 to show the president's security men where my house was. I also realized that on the afternoon of their visit, my mother, who was living with us, had left the veranda where we were sitting.

Later, she told me where she had gone.

"I noticed that something wrong must have been going on, but I didn't know what it was," she said. "I also saw that the young man living with us had walked inside the house, and he looked worried, so I went to my room."

She had been on her knees praying the entire time.

∽

Memories of my family, I have found, of those still here and others who have died, are always all around me.

Because so many of my close relatives have died, there are very few of us left. I have only one brother left living, Samy Mukekwa, who lives in Kinshasa. Samy and I were estranged for some time, but he is turning out to be a wonderful brother, especially since the death of our mother.

As Tshinabu was when I was a child, Samy is very protective of me now, especially when I go to Kinshasa. Like me, he has realized there are only the two of us left. I can always sense that he is afraid of losing me, and we now are developing a much deeper sense of love for each other.

Every day, something reminds me of a family member. Occasionally, I see something that I wish I could tell Tshinabu about, or I recognize characteristics in others that I once saw in my father or mother. For instance, my father liked to collect new plants he encountered on his travels. He would take cuttings home and try them in the soil and climate of Kajiji. Once, near Strasbourg, France, I was visiting a farm with a member of the Mennonite World Conference executive committee, Hugo Moriera. Hugo saw several plants that interested him on the farm and asked if he could take a sample home to Uruguay. Like Hugo, my father was always willing to try new things in new places, in hopes of seeing new life take root and grow.

When our daughter, Annie, got married recently, we had a wonderful wedding in the mountains near Yosemite National Park. Twice during the ceremony, I was very moved by what was happening because it reminded me of how short and fragile life can be. When the minister asked who was giving Annie in marriage to her new husband, Brian, I answered that it was not only Linda and I, but our extended family. I felt very alone at that moment, wishing my parents and other siblings could have been there. I began to weep.

Annie had decided we would light a candle during the wedding reception to honor family members who had passed on. This simple act, the lighting of a candle, also brought me to tears. Again, I felt terribly alone.

During the celebrations of Christmas 2008, which Linda and I spent with the Heinrichses, my American family, I reflected on my life and recalled a few important facts.

In June 2008, I turned 56. The following month marked 32 years since the car accident that left me partially paralyzed. Instead of dwelling on this, and on the fact that my American parents are now in their 80s, the age when my biological parents died, and that I still live with a great deal of physical pain, I am very thankful.

Our daughter, Patience, now a graduate of Fresno Pacific, recently told me, "Dad, everywhere I go, I find someone who knows you."

Likewise, I find echoes of my parents, and of me, in those who gather around me today.

When we were back in Kinshasa in 2007, Samba, the daughter of my late sister, Suzanne, asked me if we could talk in private. In my room, she handed me an envelope and said, "This is the salary from my second month of work. I wanted you to have it." I opened the envelope and it had the equivalent of $15. That was all she had, but she wanted to give it all to me. I cried as I held the envelope in my hand. I hugged her and blessed her. I felt the presence of both my mother and my sister in that room. Just like my mother, Samba gave everything she had without question.

When he was a little boy, my nephew, Jean Pululu, Suzanne's oldest son, wanted to be a mechanic, just as I had once. However, he is now completing medical school in Kinshasa. Does he have the ambition of being a great surgeon? I don't know. Time will tell.

Annie's niece, Naomi, now six years old, is playing soccer and wants to be like me, her grandpa. Oh, how family history repeats itself.

I have had a good life. Despite my disability, God granted me a home away from home, and a career that has taken me all over the world.

My friend and mentor Dalton Reimer recently told me that he thought I have a lot left to do.

"I think your best days are ahead," he told me. "You have many things going for you, Pakisa. People trust you and you have gained respect of many people around the world. How are you going to put it to a good use?"

While I was pondering Dalton's question, in January 2009, I wept as I watched Barack Obama sworn in as the first African-American president of the United States. That evening, I joined a large group gathered at the African American Museum in Fresno to celebrate the inauguration. An African-American historian in attendance said he felt that he was now truly American.

Though Dalton didn't really expect me to answer, I saw his question for what it is. Indeed, this question was really a challenge, one I will try to meet for as long as I am able.